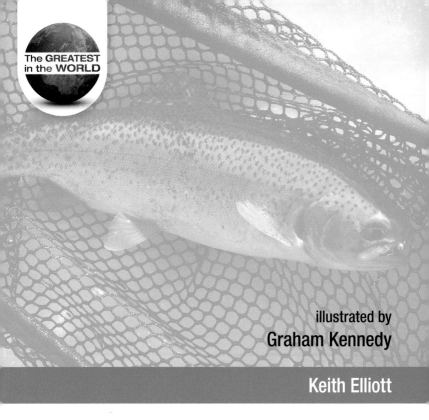

illustrated by
Graham Kennedy

Keith Elliott

The Greatest
Fishing
Tips in the World

A 'The Greatest in the World' book

www.thegreatestintheworld.com

Illustrations:
Graham Kennedy

Typesetting:
BR Typesetting

Cover images:
© Flyfisherman; © Klikk; © Mikearicha; © Gina Smith
all courtesy of www.fotolia.com

Copy editor:
Bronwyn Robertson
www.theartsva.com

Series creator/editor:
Steve Brookes

Published in 2008 by
The Greatest in the World Ltd, PO Box 3182,
Stratford-upon-Avon, Warwickshire CV37 7XW

Text and Illustrations Copyright © 2008 – The Greatest in the World Ltd.

A CIP catalogue record for this book is available from the British Library
ISBN 978-1-905151-33-2

Printed and bound in China by 1010 Printing International Ltd.

To Amber and Fleur,
who will one day be glad that
they can tell the difference between
a roach and a rudd. Perhaps.

Contents

> **"Patience is a word invented by dull buggers who can't think fast enough."**
>
> *Spike Milligan*

A few words from Keith …

Non-anglers assume fishermen are the world's most patient people. Well, it's true that plenty of those you see by pond, river and beach are happy enough just being there. For them, a fish is an accidental bonus. Almost two-thirds go fishing to get away from it all, so research claims.

This book is not for the angler I met on the Thames, who didn't have a bait on his hook because he didn't want to keep pulling his line in and out. It's not for experts, especially now that fishing has become so segmented, with many anglers pursuing just one sort of fish (and in some cases, just one particular fish).

But if you're one of the millions who go fishing for the pleasure of it, someone who catches a few but would like to catch more, this book should give you some useful tips, wherever and however you fish. It's especially for those who want to see a little more action: those who are not content just to stare at a motionless float or rod tip all day.

Patience? Yes, it's a vital part of fishing. It's no use expecting to catch something within minutes of casting out, every time you go. That would make fishing boring. But if you're willing to try something new, to put on a bait you haven't used before, fish a different style or just do something out of the ordinary, this book will help you catch more.

Tight lines!

Keith

I love fishing. You put that line in the water and you don't know what's on the other end. Your imagination is under there.

Robert Altman

Coarse fishing

chapter 1
Coarse fishing

Use the line clip for accuracy

Most modern reels have a line clip, a slot on the spool that you can slip the line behind. While it's useful to stop line spilling off the spool, it's even more valuable for ensuring that you cast to exactly the same spot. Make sure you clip up when the leger, float, or feeder has settled, rather than when it hits the water. But be attentive with large fish like carp that can often bolt suddenly. They can break your line before you've moved, so unless the carp are small, you might feel safer marking the line with Tipp-Ex or quick-drying float paint to make sure you're casting accurately.

Quick tip

NIGHT'S THE TIME FOR EELS

Want to catch eels? You'll get a lot more at night, especially when there is little or no moon. Put them back afterwards, because a big eel can be more than 60 years old. John Sidley, one of the most successful eel fishermen, used to kill and eat every eel he caught until he checked the age of one big fish and found it was 65 years old. "I never killed another eel after that," he said. "It was like killing a pensioner."

Water comes second

Many anglers find that their groundbait is too runny. That's because they add the groundbait to water, rather than the other way around. Add small amounts, rather than a container-full, then mix. When it's getting sticky, leave for at least 10 minutes so it can absorb the water. A cheap aerosol spray will stop it drying out on hot days, though it's worth covering it with a damp cloth too.

Save money on casters

Casters, which are the chrysalis stage of a maggot, are a terrific bait. They are much cheaper to prepare yourself, rather than buying. It's easy to make a sieve (use a one-eighth mesh). You want maggot that are about to turn (the black food spot inside them that you see on fresh maggots will have gone). Run them through each day, and as soon as they start turning, do it twice or three times a day. Pick off the skins and dead maggots. These will only sour your casters.

I keep mine in a bait box with a plastic bag over them, then put on the lid. It's fine to add fresh casters that are turning to older ones, but replace the plastic bag. Don't keep them in water. When you're ready to fish, put them in a plastic bag and squeeze out the air.

Put them in water when you're ready to fish and pick out the floaters. Keep them separate. They can be effective when a sinking caster is not working, and are good on weedy bottoms. Floaters can also work when big roach are picking casters off the top. Using different shades can often be very effective. On some days, a dark caster works best; on others, it's the light ones.

Try wheat for bait

You don't have to spend a fortune on boilies, casters and maggots. One very effective and very cheap bait for roach and chub is wheat. You can buy it very cheaply at corn chandlers or places selling bird food. A cupful will last you all day. Leave in water overnight (you can add flavourings here) then boil it. It's ready when it starts to split. You need to feed wheat sparsely because it's very filling, but it seems to tempt much larger roach. It works best in summer and autumn.

PAINT YOUR BOXES

Most anglers carry several boxes. Put a blob of paint on the lid in different colours. This helps you to identify which is which on the bank and when the light is starting to fade.

Look for drop-offs to find pike

The secret of locating pike is locating their prey. If you're in a boat, this is very easy because an echo-sounder will help you locate shoals of roach and other fish. It's not so easy from the bank. One very good bet is to look for sharp drop-offs. The pike will move between the deep and shallower water, though you will probably catch them in the latter. To locate such spots, go round the water you intend to fish with a plummet. Pike will come up quite a long way to take a bait or lure. I've found that fishing 2 m (6 ft) deep in 4 m (12 ft) of water is just as effective as fishing on the bottom.

Quick tip

DIFFERENT WAYS WITH MEAT

Luncheon meat is very effective on heavily stocked waters, especially those with a large head of carp. But after a while, the fish wise up to cubes of it. That's when you need to get smart. Try using two pieces of meat, using a smaller piece or breaking it by hand to get uneven shapes. Other alternatives are flavouring or colouring it. You'll be surprised how often the change will make a big difference. Another possibility is making a paste with it. You can mix it with a proprietary paste, or add a little liquidised bread to stiffen it. But don't be worried if it seems very soft. Carp and tench seem to prefer softer baits.

Dealing with line bites

On heavily fished waters, you will often experience a lot of 'line bites' where fish bump into the line. This can also happen when you are legering for bream. If you strike at these false bites, you can spook the fish, or foul-hook them. Even top anglers can't always tell the difference, and carp especially will feel a line across their backs, bolt away and pull the hook in to their body or fins.

If you are legering, try casting a yard or so shorter. It's probable that the fish are feeding between you and your baited hook. But cast slightly offline to avoid landing a feeder or lead right in the middle of a feeding shoal. With bream and carp, you should generally wait until the tip pulls right round. This will stop you striking at false bites.

Ways to avoid foul-hooking carp

On the float, line bites often occur because there are just too many fish in the swim. Stop feeding, or feed much more lightly. If you are fishing for shoal carp on the float, take a little weight off the line so your float is not dotted right down. This will stop you striking at every dip of the float. If you are fishing for carp on the top, lighter feeding may help, or you may find it pays to wait until the elastic on your pole whizzes out or the fish takes line off the reel.

Foul-hooked fish are much harder to land. Try to play them clear of where you are fishing, and play them a lot harder if the fish is of an average size and you don't mind if it comes off. Often, if the hook is in a fin, it will sometimes come free with heavy pressure. Then again, you might want to land the fish because it's an exceptional one, so play it more lightly than you would normally.

Add a touch of plastic

Spinning for pike, perch, zander, or even chub? Then add a plastic worm tail to your lure or spinner. These are very cheap and come in different sizes. Choose a size to fit your quarry and lure. For perch, you can even cut these tails into strips. Changing colours can make quite a difference. It doesn't have to make the lure colour: often, a contrasting tail seems to produce better results. Keep these plastic baits separate from your normal tackle and in their sealable bags, or they will glue themselves to other tackle and become unusable.

Keep that soft paste on the hook

If your paste baits always seem to fall off, use a cable tie. Attach it close to the bottom of your rod or pole and hook the line over it. Make sure the bait is only a few inches from the tie. Swing the rod or pole out underarm, then turn it to release the bait.

Alcohol is no winter warmer

The idea that alcohol will warm you when winter or night fishing is false. You're much better taking a flask with a hot drink or soup. Alcohol also slows your senses and will make you sleepy.

Fridge your maggots

Maggots are still one of the best all-round baits. They will keep much longer in a fridge than in your baitbox, so fridge any unused baits when you've finished fishing. If your mother, wife, or girlfriend isn't too keen on maggots sharing the family fridge, get your own. Put it in a garage or shed. You can buy used ones very cheaply and it will save you buying fresh bait all the time. But don't forget to defrost regularly!

Give maggots a good clean

Once you've bought your maggots, run them through a sieve to get out all the skins, dead maggots, and waste that sometimes comes with the bait. Then use a finer sieve to take off the sawdust, and put the bait in maize meal. (Indian shops are a good place to buy this.) This cleans their skins, helping them to sink, and takes away the ammonia smell. I add a little turmeric.

Izaak Walton's 1653 *The Compleat Angler* has gone into more editions than any other book except the works of Shakespeare and the Bible.

AN OLD SECRET

Old maggots are good if you're catching a lot of fish and don't want to keep changing the bait, especially for dace and bleak, or on heavily stocked waters where you might be pestered by fish like roach, rudd, and small bream.

Floating maggots

If you want to catch fish on the drop, riddle off any maize meal and put a handful of maggots on a bait box with a square cut out of the lid; (that will stop them crawling out). Put in just enough water to cover the maggots. Within 30 minutes, you will have a maggot that will float. These are very effective as a change bait, or when you are fishing on the drop.

Firing maggots in the wind

Want to feed maggots at distance, but the wind's against you? The trouble with a catapult is that strong winds will spread the maggots everywhere. The answer is to clean your maggots as if you're preparing them as a floating bait (see above) then sprinkle Horlicks powder over them. You can buy proprietary products like Sticky Mag, but Horlicks is cheaper. The maggots can be compressed into a ball and fired substantial distances.

Single can work best

Missing pike runs? Try a single hook in the bait's lip, rather than a pair of trebles. This often works best with live baits.

Try chopped maggots too

Chopped worm is a terrific method for almost all fish, but you'll find that chopped maggots can work well too. Use a bait dropper in running water because they are lighter than worms.

Head for the sea

If you're deadbaiting for pike, sea baits often work better than the pike's regular diet of freshwater fish. Sea fish such as herring, sprats, and mackerel have more oils than freshwater fish, and they are easily obtainable. Freezing them means you always have a supply of baits, because you can be sure that when pike are feeding you just won't be able to catch roach, dace and so on! Freeze them as fresh as possible. The freshest mackerel and herrings will shine and have bright eyes. Unless you're desperate, don't buy those with the guts spilling out. They're not very fresh.

Turn a red mullet blue

Try something different with sea baits. Sardines, red mullet, even kippers will catch pike, and sections of fish like garfish can be deadly. Dye them different colours. A change can often work wonders. Try 'popping up' the bait so it's clear of the bottom, and retrieve slowly, because you will often get a take then.

Don't lose your torch

Night fishing? A head torch with several LEDs will give a bright, direct light which is better than a fixed one because you won't lose it! Carry spare batteries.

Double your bait and your runs

Try using half a mackerel or herring, rather than the whole fish. Using a kebab rig, where chunks of fish are used on a hair rig, proves very effective when other methods don't work, and it puts out a terrific scent trail.

Protect your fingers

If you're using dead baits in low light, use one semi-barbed hook on a treble, as the bait-holding hook, and two barbless ones. Put a strip of red on the barbed one to save putting it into your fingers, and so you can re-bait easily.

Tares will sort out bigger fish

Pestered by small fish when using hemp? Try tares, which can be bought from a petfood shop. Prepare them in the same ways as hemp, though they need a little more boiling to soften them. Elderberries can also sort out bigger fish. You can preserve them, and use them throughout the year. Many people stop using hemp once summer's over, but it will still catch in the depths of winter, and it's a superb attractant for all fish.

Bulk buy your hemp – but beware mice!

Save money by buying hemp in bulk, but keep it in an enclosed container because mice love it! Hemp freezes well, so simply refreeze leftover bait. Adding soda to the boiling water will make it blacker. Add a drop of food colouring (red works well) or try some of the carp flavourings, though use sparingly and flavour the night before rather than when you start fishing.

Hemp on the top

You don't have to fish hemp on or near the bottom. The biggest fish will often come to the top to take it, but they seem impossible to hook. Try using a big hook (as large as a 12 or even 10), a larger float so that the float itself helps to hook the fish, and heavier line than normal. You can catch as shallow as 30 cm (1 ft) fishing like this, but you need to pull the line, as if in fly-fishing, rather than striking, or you'll get the line knitted round your rod top.

Keeping hemp on the hook

The standard way to hook hemp is to push the hook bend into the split where the white seed is showing. But if your hooks are sharp (and they should be) you can insert the hook into the indented end of the seed and then manoeuvre the point so that it comes out in the split part. This is ideal if you are missing bites and keep losing the bait. When fish are feeding well on hemp, you can catch them on artificial hemp, or even a piece of rubber wire protector with a white core.

Quick tip

FINDING THE BEST SPOTS

Fishing a new water? You'll often find that the well-trodden swims are close to the car park. This isn't because they are the best spots, but because people are lazy! A longer walk will usually result in better fishing. Well-trodden spots well away from the car park, however, are probably a sign of a good spot.

PVA for accuracy

Want to ensure accurate feeding? Then use a PVA 'stringer'.
Thread half-boilies or pellets on, with a 2.5 cm (1 in) gap
between each so the PVA dissolves cleanly, then loop on your
hook. PVA bags can be used for accurate feeding at distance
for every bait, but keep them in a dry place or you'll just have
a ball of mush.

Quick tip

BREAK UP YOUR BOILIES

Using half-boilies distributes smell and attractants into
the water quicker. Two half-boilies are often more effective
than one whole one, especially in waters where the fish
have become wary of boilies. This is especially so of
barbel.

Braid spots the bites

Missing a lot of bites on the leger or feeder? If you wind in and
your bait's gone, or you're getting small indications that don't
turn into a proper bite, or your maggots have been crushed,
there are several things you can do. Probably the best is to use
braid line rather than monofilament. This has no stretch to it
and turns tiny indications into proper bites. But be careful on
the strike, especially if you're using small hooks and light lines.
Because braid as no stretch, it's easy to snap off. Just lifting
into a bite, even at distance, is usually enough to hook a fish.
But always use mono traces with braid main line.

Fill the spool

It's amazing the number of anglers who don't fill a fixed-spool reel correctly. It should be filled almost to the rim of the spool. It will mean you need to put less effort into your casting and you'll cast farther. It also means line comes off the reel more smoothly if you're playing a big fish.

Backwinding big fish

Some anglers like to flick off the anti-reverse and play big fish by backwinding. It's certainly more sensitive, but with very big fish you're better off using the slipping clutch adjustment. Set it for the fish you intend to catch. Roach and dace, fished with 1 kg (2 lb) line, will need a far lighter setting than if you're targeting barbel, carp, and chub with 3.5 kg (8 lb) main line.

No need for rethreading

There's nothing more annoying when using a fixed-spool than threading line through your rod rings, only to find that you haven't flicked the bail arm over. (You only seem to find out when you've set up all your terminal tackle too.) It doesn't mean you have to rethread the rod again. Simply remove the spool, flick the bail arm over and all's well.

Silicon, not plastic

Don't use plastic sleeves to hold on your float. These will damage high-tech lines. Always use silicon rubber, which is much softer. Use three lengths of rubber, rather than two. It will stop the float slipping and if one breaks, you can still fish on.

Top 10

biggest fish in the record list

1 2664lb great white

2 1785lb 11oz tiger shark

3 1708lb 9oz Greenland shark

4 1560lb black marlin

5 1402lb 2oz Atlantic blue marlin

6 1376lb Pacific blue marlin

7 1221lb shortfin mako shark

8 1298lb six-gilled shark

9 1280lb hammerhead shark

10 1496lb bluefin tuna

Changing the colour

Silicon rubber has other benefits. As light changes, you will often find is nearly impossible to see your float. Just slip over a length of dark or light silicon, depending on conditions. It saves you having to keep changing floats.

Play it softly

Using bite alarms? For the sake of everyone else on the lake, don't use the most sensitive setting. Wind and drifting weed will give you lots of false bites, and nearby anglers will want to drown you for that alarm screeching every five minutes (especially at night!). With modern bolt rigs, carp rarely give subtle bites. But if you're after shy-biting big roach, slack lines and light bobbins will enhance bites when legering in stillwater. Use long drops if you're using indicators, to avoid striking at line bites.

Hair rig for all species

Almost all carp anglers now use a hair rig. But you can use it with most other species and catch more. You don't have to leger it, either. It's equally effective on the float, and yields more bites for fish like tench, chub, bream and even pike and roach. Varying the hair length can make quite a difference but the general lesson is: very short is best.

Light and dark fish

Big bream and big rudd feed best when light levels are falling. Perch and pike, on the other hand, feed better during daytime (though this doesn't mean you won't catch them at night).

Quick tip

DEADBAIT FOR CHUB
Big stillwater chub will often fall for a small deadbait like a bleak or a minnow.

Bottom-only for wagglers

Using a waggler? This should always be connected bottom-only. But don't just put the line through the bottom ring. Always use a quick-change attachment that will fold over on the strike. It also means that if the wind gets up you can quickly put on a heavier float, rather than setting it all up again. Putting the bulk of your shot under the float works best, but don't attach them tight to the connector. Leave about a 1¼ cm (half-inch) gap.

Sinking the line

You'll generally want your line to sink when using a waggler. Ask your tackle dealer for a main line that sinks, and once the float has hit the water, put your rod top below the surface, give the line a flick, as if striking, to sink the line, then wind it so there is a straight line between float and rod tip. When it's very windy, keep your rod tip below the surface to beat drift.

You need a stop shot for sliders

When using a sliding float, don't have the float sliding on to your bulk shot. Put a smaller shot above this and you will get far fewer tangles. Many anglers are frightened of deep water and automatically use a leger or feeder. But a slider is very effective, especially if fish are feeding on the drop.

Button up your sticks

The classic way to shot a stick float is to string out the shot, called 'shirt-buttoning'. Make sure that your shots are in descending order of size, with the smallest shots nearest the hook. If you're fishing a heavy stick float, it's better to use two No.4s than a No.1. It allows you to make finer adjustments. Many top float anglers will use all No.8s for this reason. With smaller shot (No.8s downwards), you can also use lead weights which are much softer than tungsten, or lead-free so you can move them on the line with less damage.

Sticks floats need a floating line

Use a floating line on a stick float. You can buy a spray to do this, or use diluted washing-up liquid to make your line float. If wind is blowing your stick float off course, use a back shot, which is a shot between the rod top and float. In really fierce wind, you can use a couple of backshot as large as BB.

Supermarkets can save the day

Forgotten your bait and the tackle shop is closed? Don't worry. There are masses of potential baits at your local supermarket, and these often stay open all night. Try jelly, peperami, Sugar Puffs, mini-marshmallows, chick peas, and pearl barley, as well as the obvious ones like corn, bread, and meat. Steak is a great chub bait (use it with mince, but feed sparingly). Pastas, including macaroni and spaghetti, will catch everything from carp to roach, though they need cooking. You can use small pieces to catch silver fish, or a whole ravioli or some of those exotic pasta shapes for carp, tench, and chub.

Shimano is the only manufacturer to have achieved 3000 world records on its tackle.

Stopping the caster thieves

When fishing casters, check that the end of the bait hasn't been nipped and the juices sucked out. If this happens frequently, thread your hook right inside the caster rather than hooking it through the end. When hooking meat or sweetcorn, make sure the hook point protrudes.

Watch the crawlers

When hooking maggots, you will notice that they crawl with their tiny extension or 'mouth' underneath. Nick the hook beneath their skin so they can crawl naturally, or you will find that the maggot turns over and impedes the hook, losing you fish. When using double maggot, you will find that the line twists a lot more. Use a tiny swivel to join hooklength to main line, and try hooking one maggot in the head, the other in the tail. Changing from a single maggot to a double will often bring a larger fish.

Get spare tips for a pole

Many anglers use a pole for stillwater fishing. You may think you need one of 16 m (50 ft): you don't. For most pleasure fishing 11 m (35 ft) is fine, though you should try to buy one with spare tops so you can rig up with differing strengths of elastic. If you want extra length, you can buy an additional universal section fairly cheaply. If you regularly fish a place susceptible to wind, buy a stiffish pole. There's a reason that some poles cost more than others, and it's usually weight and stiffness that add to the price.

Feed to keep them interested

Many anglers make the key mistake of failing to feed regularly.
Get in the habit of feeding every cast or every fish, even if it's
only a few maggots, a pinch of hemp or a couple of mini-boilies
or pellets. Learn to hold your rod or pole with one hand and
feed with the other. Match anglers will keep feeding even when
playing a fish so a shoal does not drift off.

Back your tackle dealer

Support your local shop. If you buy all your big items by mail
order or online, you'll find the handy local shop suddenly goes
out of business, and you'll have to travel a lot farther to buy
those little bits like hooks, weights, and bait. Most local shops
will do their best to match (or come close to) mail order prices,
and supporting them will save you a lot more in the long run.

Quick tip

SUPERGLUE IS A SUPER AID

A tube of Superglue is a very handy thing for your tackle
box. When going for big fish, I always add a dab to my
hook knot for extra security. But it can also save you if,
for example, a rod whipping comes adrift.

Peg down that brolly

If you're fishing in inclement weather and using an umbrella,
carry some string and tent pegs for extra security, unless you
want to watch your umbrella flying across the water.

Deter the tackle jackals

There's nothing worse than going fishing at night, settling into your bivvy and waking up in the morning to discover that tackle jackals have stolen your kit while you slept. A night-fishing sensor light is a sensible investment. They are very cheap and you can position two or three to cover all areas.

A bivvy with a clear front also means you can see what's happening in front of you. Bivvy slippers are a good idea to save you running on a muddy bank in bare feet and trying to put on boots in the dark.

Barbless is best

Don't be frightened of using barbless hooks. They penetrate better and make unhooking far easier. If you're playing fish properly, keeping a tight line, you won't lose them because the hook doesn't have a barb. Many waters now insist on barbless hooks. Always carry a couple of disgorgers. It's easy to drop one in the water and lose it.

Forceps help with unhooking

For bigger fish, carry a set of long-nosed forceps. These will help you remove hooks from tough-mouthed fish like carp and barbel, and will means you won't end up with bleeding hands if you're trying to remove hooks from a deep-hooked pike.

Try the upside-down quill

A brilliant method on stillwaters for shy-biting fish is the upside-down crowquill. The buoyancy is in the thicker end, so the thin end is ultra-sensitive. You can catch fish with this method by using a shot only an inch or so from the hook. Overshot the float and adjust the depth until the float is standing up straight. Most of your bites will be lift bites, with the float laying flat as a fish picks up the bait.

Quick tip

TRAVEL LIGHT AND FREELINE

One of the best methods for big fish on rivers is to freeline a bait. It means you can travel light and cover a lot of water. Baits like worms, meat and cheese have a natural weight, and will travel easily through a swim.

Landing crucian carp

If you seem to lose a lot of crucian carp, try this. The moment the fish is hooked, put hardly any pressure on during its first run. After that, you'll find you can tighten up and it will probably stay on.

Long-casting meat

Want to cast meat long distances? It always seems to come off, doesn't it? Then try the Fox stop and sleeve system, which keeps the meat intact and allows you to fish at distance. You can also freeze the meat, which stays on in casting but unfreezes in the water.

If people concentrated on the really important things in life, there'd be a shortage of fishing rods.

Doug Larson

Top 10

fish that you've probably never heard of
(but are listed in the International Game Fish
Association records)

1	Bigmouth buffalo	70lb 5oz
2	Giant African threadfin	99lb 3oz
3	Guinean snapper	103lb 9oz
4	Nembwe	5lb 2oz
5	Pirambeba	5lb
6	Rohu	27lb 8oz
7	Shorthead redhorse	8lb 12oz
8	Tambaqui	23lb
9	Tripletail	40lb 13oz
10	Wenchman	4lb 6oz

Use a mat

Always use unhooking mats with big carp, tench, catfish, barbel, and pike, and exceptional specimens of other species.

Be a fish doctor

If there are any wounds on a fish, caused by anything from cormorants to pike, keep a tube of Bonjela with you and treat the wound.

The artificial route

Fish don't seem to mind artificial maggots, corn, or casters, and they work well when fished with the real thing.

Stop pellets splitting

Do you find that hard pellets keep splitting? Use a fine drill to drill halfway through, then drill from the other side to meet the hole you've made. You'll find that pellets smaller than 12 mm (½ in) tend to split anyway. Try using a band with these.

Bread for big roach

Want to catch big roach? The most successful bait is plain old bread. An unsliced fresh loaf gives you the choice of using a buoyant bait like crust or a sinking bait by using flake. Press the bread around the hook shank, but leave the bit around the hook fluffy. It's undoubtedly the best bait for big roach and chub on a clear river in winter. At these times, the biggest specimens always stay at the back of the shoal. You can cast further downstream, or cast offline and hold the float back to miss the smaller fish at the head of a shoal.

Watch your watch

Buy a fishing watch, like the ones made by Casio. They are not a gimmick. If you can understand the instructions, you'll find they are very effective when it comes to the best times to fish, especially if coupled with checking water temperature and barometric pressure.

Layer to keep warm in winter

Fishing in winter? Take more warm clothes than you need. You can easily take clothes off, but you can't put them on if you haven't got them. On frosty banks, moon boots are invaluable for keeping your feet warm. Always wear a hat because so much heat is lost through the head. Layers are better than one thick sweater.

Clothing back-up

Have a spare set of clothes in your car in case you fall in, and always carry a spare pair of socks. There are few things worse than fishing in winter with wet feet.

Travel warnings

Taking tackle on holiday with you? The range of travel rods that will fit in your suitcase now covers everything from carp rods to heavyweights for beach-casting. Otherwise you need a specialist rod carrier, which is always a hassle at airports. Don't take any hooks, line, lures (unless without hooks) or even reels in your hand baggage. There's every chance they will be confiscated, though how you could be a danger with a packet of hooks escapes me.

Moving maggots

Fishing in Denmark, Holland, Ireland, or somewhere that requires a lot of maggots? Chill them almost to freezing, pack them tight in a cold box and add ice packs. Seal tightly. They will travel for a couple of days in this state of suspended animation.

Change the hooks

Travelling abroad to somewhere that means mainly lure fishing? Cut down on the weight and space by taking all the trebles off and retackling when you arrive. For fish like mahseer and Nile perch, and most big-game sea species, don't even bother to take ordinary trebles. Their jaws are so strong they will crush ordinary hooks. Take extra-strong ones, like those made by Owner.

Quick tip

BAD MIXERS
Never mix worms and maggots in the same box. You'll kill off the worms.

Buy lures in the US

If you're going on holiday to the US, leave some space in your bag for lures. They are half the price you pay in Europe, and places like Wal-Mart often have them reduced even further. But don't carry them in your hand baggage because you won't be allowed to carry them on the plane. Quite how you're going to hold up a plane with a spinner, I'm not sure, but rules are rules...

When barbel come to visit

If you're catching roach and dace on a river that's known for barbel, and suddenly things go quiet, there's every chance that a barbel (of course, it could be a pike!) has moved in. Push the float up 60 cm (2 ft), add a couple of extra large, say, BB, shot about 30 cm (1 ft) from the hook and hold back the float hard. With small (1.5-3 kg/3-6 lb) barbel, you can catch several fish like this. Barbel are less inclined to chase a bait through the swim, and by laying-on, you are less likely to foulhook one.

Watch out for the taxman

Buying lures and other tackle that's cheaper in the US through the internet (from places like Bass Pro Shops or Cabela's) seems a sensible idea. But when it's imported into another country, you can be hit for an extra 20 per cent or more over various taxes if customs spots your package. That can take away all the money you thought that you'd saved. The same applies to buying new tackle through eBay. If it costs under £25, there's no tax to pay. Of course, it would be irresponsible of me to suggest you ask the seller to declare its value at £25 (every export must carry a customs declaration form).

Check the mesh

Don't put barbel in keepnets, and make sure your net is of an approved mesh. Many people inherit tackle such as keepnets, and the old-style mesh is terribly damaging to fish, taking off their scales and lacerating their fins.

Help the kids

Be patient with children fishing near you. Giving them help is very rewarding. Show them how to set up properly, give them a few hooks and floats, and turn them into anglers for life.

Quick tip

DRIVE THEM WILD WITH RED
Predators are attracted by the colour red. Cut out pieces of soft plastic and attach one (or two) to your trebles. This works with deadbaits and livebaits too, not just for spinning. You'll also find it's successful for perch and chub.

The right way to unhook a pike

Scared of unhooking pike because of their sharp teeth? Handle them properly and you won't get bitten. Unless you're totally confident about 'chinning' a fish, use a net. (Never, ever, use a gaff, whatever they say in the old books.) Take the fish out and put it on an unhooking mat. You may be able to take the hooks out easily if it's lightly hooked, or if you're just using a single hook. Otherwise, trap the fish between your knees and remove the hooks with long-nosed forceps.

If one of the hooks has gone deep, turn over the pike and, gripping it under its jaw, lift the fish's head slightly to find the trebles. You have to feed your forceps through the gill cover to loosen a treble that is lodged in the throat. Do this very carefully so you don't damage the gill rakers.

Don't go for gold

Tempted to use goldfish as a pike bait? Don't. The problem is that while they show up wonderfully in the water, there's every chance that they carry koi herpes virus (KHV) or some other disease. Most of the goldfish in this country are not bred here but in countries like Israel, where the warmer weather makes them grow more quickly.

You might think that freezing them would get rid of any disease, but viruses can be kept alive by freezing. Be safe, not sorry. You could wreck a fishery by careless action.

If you really want to use a deadbait that stands out, try some of the more exotic sea fish that you regularly see on fish counters, especially the ethnic ones. Red ones like snapper and mullet seems to work well. I cut off the spiky fins but I don't think it makes any difference. After all, pike eat perch and ruffe!

Paint your deadbaits

You can also use special paint to colour a deadbait. I bought some stuff called Spectra Minnow in the US at Cabela's, and it comes in a range of colours, from orange and red to green, blue, chartreuse (which seems to be the best of all) and yellow.

Tweak for a bite

Can't get a bite? Use the matchman's trick and move your bait. You don't need to pull it out of the water; just a tweak can make all the difference. It works for almost all species, but it's particularly effective for bream and carp. It's also deadly when fishing a deadbait for pike. Move the bait just a few inches because pike sense the vibrations and it imitates a dying fish.

Fact

The World Worm Charming Championship is held at Nantwich every June. This is a unique event where worms 'charmed' out of the soil by over 200 competitors from around the world. The record was set by Tom Shufflebotham in 1980 when he charmed 511 worms out of the ground at the first ever World Worm Charming Championship.

fantastic

> My biggest worry is that my wife (when I'm dead) will sell my fishing gear for what I said I paid for it.

Koos Brandt

Travel cheaply…

If you're lucky enough to afford a trip for the Indian mahseer, Spanish catfish or even to fish one of the big-fish lakes like Bung Sam Lan in Thailand, you don't need ultra-expensive rods. In many cases, you will be using hefty uptide rods, and in places where there are a lot of rocks or where you're clambering around, a £200 carbon rod can easily get damaged. I use cheap uptiders, costing less than £40. They might not look as good, but they do the job well and stand up far better to the rigours of being thrown around. And if you're unlucky enough to get them stolen you won't be quite so distressed!

… but not with this kit

Don't skimp on reels, line and hooks. Even though the cheapest modern reels are way better than a typical quality reel of 30 years ago, you will find it a false economy to take the low-cost route. Big fish, from tarpon to catfish, will test these items to the maximum and you could end up losing the fish of a lifetime.

Quick tip

KEEP AWAY FROM PYLONS

Don't fish under electricity pylons, however tempting a swim might be. Almost all electricity pylons over water now carry a warning, but many anglers still think that if they use a rod or pole that will not touch the power cable, they are safe. Not true. Electricity can 'jump' quite a distance. It's also a wise bet to put down a carbon rod or pole when there's lightning about.

Record your catch…

Digital cameras are now so cheap and light that every angler should carry one. The great thing about them is that you can see if the picture has come out well, and the quality is far higher than you will get with a mobile phone. When you take a photo of a fish, try to put something in the picture (besides the fish) that gives an idea of its size. A reel will always give an idea of size.

…because it may win you a prize

If you catch an exceptional fish, try to get someone else to take the photo. Might seem obvious, but I'm amazed at the number of anglers who have someone else holding the fish they've caught because they don't trust someone else with their camera. Having another angler holding your fish isn't much of a memory, is it? If you're looking to enter the fish in weekly or monthly competitions run by angling magazines or websites, you will need a quality photo and witnesses. Try to get someone else other than your brother or best friend.

One for the record

If you're lucky enough to catch a fish that could be a record, you will need several photographs, especially if it's a fish like a rudd, roach, bream or dace, or perhaps one of the many species of jack, so that it can be definitely identified by an expert. You should also measure the fish's length and its girth, and if you are returning the fish, make sure that you have two or three independent witnesses carrying out the weighing. You then need to get the scales checked as quickly as possible by your local weights and measures office.

If you're making a claim for a world record, you need to check the procedure of the International Game Fish Association (IGFA) at **www.igfa.org**. You have to make claims within 60 days of the catch and supply a length of the line used. You might think: "I'll never set a world record", but as well as all-tackle records, the IGFA accepts claims for different line strengths right down to 2 lb, as well as fly-caught records with different strength tippets. Many of these records are open, and not just for obscure fish. (For example, all the grayling line-class records are vacant.) There are also categories for juniors (under 16) small fry (under 12) and a whole set of separate records for fish caught by women.

Stay away from the water

Never drink water from the place where you're fishing without boiling it, even if the locals claim it's fine. In some places, it should go through a water filter too.

This is because there are some incredibly nasty things that lurk in water. At very least, you could end up with diarrhoea, dysentery or typhoid.

One of the biggest dangers on the bankside is Weil's disease or leptospirosis, and it's carried in rats' urine. (Still want to drink that water?) It's very nasty and can even kill you, and you can catch it from infected water entering a cut, or even by touching the bank and then eating food.

There's even a disease called beaver fever (giardiasis) that can be caused by drinking infected water. Though beavers are among the hosts, it can also be carried by dogs, cats, horses, and cattle. The best bet is to take your drinks with you!

Beating the bugs

Bugs can take away the pleasure from even the most prolific fishing venue. Places like Russia, Canada and even Scotland can be unbearable because of blackfly, midges and mosquitoes – and they seem to turn up just when the fishing's at its best.

Mosquitoes in particular can also be dangerous, carrying not just malaria but dengue fever, encephalitis, yellow fever and Nile fever. None is very nice and some could kill you. If you're fishing places where the mosquitoes carry these diseases (check on **www.traveldoctor.co.uk** or with your local doctor), make sure you've had the correct injections or you're taking anti-malarial tablets. When you see someone who's got malaria, you won't even think about saving money by not taking the tablets.

Prevention is better than cure, and many anglers swear by Avon's Skin So Soft, though its effectiveness as a repellent doesn't last very long unless you use the one with a Deet-free pesticide in it. There is a shirt marketed by Nomad (**www. nomaduk.net**) that claims to keep mosquitoes and ticks away and works well.

In some places, you will need to wear a face net, spray a Deet product (I use 100 per cent Deet, but I'm told it can affect some people's skin) and ensure there are not places where they can land and bite. One forgotten (and very itchy area) is your ankles. Wear thick socks or ankle-covering boots.

If you're fishing a beach where there are sandflies, you will save yourself a great deal of trouble by wearing socks. Doesn't look good, but it will save you those incredibly itchy bites around your ankles. In some places, sandfly carry leishmaniasis, which in its worst forms can cause skin lesions that resemble leprosy, or even kill you.

Mosquito coils are very effective at night, though some people can't stand the smell and I'm sure breathing their contents can't be terribly good for you. I always carry a pack, though. Light them before you eat or go to bed to kill all mosquitoes.

The biggest problem, though, often comes after being bitten. It's easy to scratch away at night, and awake to find that you have a raw wound that is twice as itchy. The answer here is a Zanza-Klick (though there are various other proprietary names). It's a pocket-sized device that emits an electrical impulse, and it makes a huge difference after you've been bitten.

Just put it on a bite, click it nine or ten times, and it will not only reduce the swelling but ease the itching. You may have to use it a few times, but I wouldn't travel anywhere that mosquitoes could be a nuisance without one.

I've just been sent some patches that are Deet-free and are said to keep away biting insects for 36 hours. Can't vouch for the efficiency or otherwise of Natural Patches, but if the smell or the chemicals in Deet worry you, they're worth a try.

There will be days when the fishing is better than one's most optimistic forecast, others when it is far worse. Either is a gain over just staying home.

Roderick Haig-Brown

Carp fishing

chapter 2
Carp fishing

Take a different route

On many waters that are heavily stocked, you need to use bigger baits to attract larger carp. Boilies are boiled paste baits, usually combinations of fishmeals, milk proteins, bird foods, semolina, and soya flour, which are mixed with eggs as a binding agent and then boiled to form hardish round baits which will last in the water. The round shape allows the baits to be catapulted accurately when fishing at range.

It's often impossible to get through the 2¼-3 kg (5-7 lb) fish if you're using small boilies. On such waters, the only way is to use very large boilies, even a couple of these. But on waters with lower-density stocking, where you're not getting a run every five minutes (and after a while, who wants that?) different tactics are often required to tempt fish that have seen it all, or where there is an abundance of natural food. Many anglers think the answer is to put in more rod hours, which may be the case. But think smart. Try things that the carp haven't seen before. Using corn, fishing the margins, bunches of maggots, or Sugar Puffs can produce surprising results.

Don't be hidebound and fish the same way because that's what everyone does on a particular water. Is it any surprise that all the fish are caught on the same method or bait, if everyone is fishing it? When you're fishing two, three, or four rods, use one of them to try something out of the ordinary. Small baits will often catch very big carp too.

Rats can kill

Rats are an ever-present danger for carp anglers, because Weil's disease can kill you. At least 20 per cent of feral rats carry the disease (in some areas, it's said to be as high at 90 per cent) and it comes from their urine. Catching it can be as simple as your hand, which might have a small cut, brushing the ground. The bacteria are very small, and so even a drop of water can carry millions of them, and the slightest cut could put you at risk. Carry some hand sanitiser (Daiwa sells it). Its foam kills any bacteria. It's a good idea to put a plaster and some antiseptic cream on such wounds.

It's certainly better than getting even a mild form of the disease, which can mean fever and nausea, plus fatigue and depression for some months afterwards. More severe forms can mean intensive care in hospital and even death. Drinking lake or river water is very hazardous. Always carry fresh water with you. Swimming is also very dangerous because there's no way to prevent some water getting into your body.

A pike of 90lb 8oz,
68in long, is reputed
to have been caught
in Lough Derg,
Limerick, in 1862.

Fresh is best

All boilies are best used fresh. Don't leave your packs open on the bank. (You'll never do it again if you reach out for them in the dark and touch a rat instead.) Keep the packs closed and sealed to preserve the flavours.

When carp get smart

Carp on heavily fished waters quickly learn about baits and methods that spell danger. That's the time you need to adjust your rigs. Try wrapping paste round a boilie, or using lead-free wire to give your baits a neutral balance. You can watch feeding fish flick baits with their tail to see if it behaves naturally. Doing something a little different can bring bonus fish. Another trick to add buoyancy is to use a plastic bait like a piece of corn. Tying rather than piercing a boilie prolongs its buoyancy.

Look around

Don't just watch your alarms. Look out and around the water. Put some baits in the margins, and see if they have disappeared in the morning, or even better, if there are signs of feeding fish close in.

Beware tufted ducks

Another good reason to look out, rather than down, is to keep an eye open for ducks. Most of them will stay shallow, even when they dive down. That generally isn't a problem, unless you're using floating baits. But tufted ducks are another matter. They can dive deep and clean up your feed. You may need to rebait totally (and preferably, when they are not in the vicinity!).

Learn your lines

Many anglers use just one line. Learn the qualities of different lines: floating braid and sinking braid, floating and sinking mono. For example, braid will cut through most weeds but if it gets snagged, it can be the very devil to free. On the other hand, braid is very direct and will often show you the smallest bite. Carp anglers are conditioned to wait until the line streams out off your bait-runner, but sometimes striking at small lifts can bring a fish. Change all your lines annually, and if you're fishing in a place where they can get damaged by rocks or snags, then change them as soon as you feel imperfections. Failing to do so could lose you the fish of a lifetime.

Quick tip

LEARN THE SWIM WITH BRAID
Always use a braided line when you're using a marker float to 'map out' your swim. Because it has no stretch, you can feel the changes in the bottom, and where there is weed, mud or gravel areas.

Beat the weed

When you're fishing somewhere with a weedy or soft mud bottom, try breaking up boilies when you feed them, either by spodding, catapult, or bait stick. They will sink more slowly, spread their smell more quickly and don't sink out of sight. Broken boilies also spread out across a wider area because they sink randomly, rather than straight down.

" Nothing makes a fish bigger than almost being caught. "

Anon

Think before you spod

Don't automatically get out your spodding rod, whatever the water. I recently walked around Redmire, and tangled around a branch was a spod that a careless angler had cast up a tree. Now Redmire, though a legendary carp water, is not very big: it's under three acres. You can cast across it with ease. And you can certainly feed right across it with a catapult or throwing stick. This was a classic case of an angler not thinking (and rather against the spirit of Redmire too).

That said, spodding rods are an essential piece of kit for long-distance fishing, especially where bait boats are banned. Ultra-stiff rods might seem to be the right tool but you'll cast more accurately with a rod that offers more give. Always use braid line for spodding to give you distance comfortably, especially in windy conditions.

Snip it off

It might be a bit perfectionist, but I always carry a pair of very sharp scissors to cut off the trailing bit of line after I've tiered a hook. Some anglers use a lighter to do this but I worry that it could damage the main line unless you're very careful. Quality scissors will also cut braid. Try chewing through 11 kg (25 lb) of braid with your teeth (as I tend to do with mono).

Seeds will grow your catches

Mixed seeds can form a very good feed base. Partiblend, sold by Hinders, is a particularly good bet. But you must boil the seeds first; pouring boiling water over them is not enough.

Proper way to land a fish

When landing a fish, draw it over the net and then bring the net towards you. Don't lift the net out at this stage. Collapse the arms and then carry the fish wrapped in the net. Don't drag the net along the ground.

Keep it on a mat

Always use a carp mat to protect a fish when you're unhooking or weighing it, and pour water on it before putting a fish on it. (This applies to all big fish, not just carp.) Carry a fish back to the water in the landing net or a carp sack – not in your arms. It's all too easy to drop a fish and damage it. You will notice that fish sometimes carry cuts or raw areas. Carry some antiseptic. It will be invaluable if you get a cut (see above) but you can use it to treat raw and damaged areas. It's a small thank-you to the fish as well. Whatever folklore claims, rubbing up against a tench will not be as effective!

The way to weigh

When weighing a fish, make sure that the fins are folded back, not sticking out. You should use a soft weigh-sling. Don't lift the fish too high because if it struggles, you can easily drop it. The same applies when taking a picture, whether you're using a remote or delayed action, or getting a friend to take the picture.

Colour your rigs

Using coated rigs? Try green and brown or green in weed, but use one with a yellow base for gravel or sandy bottoms.

SHARPEN UP

Sharp hooks can make all the difference. Test your hook by dragging its point across your nail with light pressure. If it catches, it's sharp enough. If not, sharpen it up or change the hook. When tying a hook, make sure that the line exits on the same side as the hook point.

Bait boat etiquette

Bait boats are very good for putting out a large amount of feed very accurately – but check to make sure that the rules allow their use, and don't use them if they will interfere with other anglers. It's only politeness, if others are fishing near you, to ask if they mind you using the boat.

Get up high

You might not be able to see fish at bank level, but climbing a tree will put you above the water and show you a lot more. Carry binoculars and polarising glasses. It's even better if you can do this sort of thing the day before, because that can save a lot of time if you're only planning a shortish session.

It's common angling courtesy not to plonk your kit down right next to the only other angler fishing on the lake. If the swims are fairly close and a water is busy, ask any adjacent angler if he minds and where he is casting to, and don't fish on his feed.

Think before you fish

All too many anglers head for a known swim and drop in there without thinking about conditions. On heavily fished waters, sometimes you don't have much of a choice. But if you get the chance, the best thing you can do is to walk right around the water, using your powers of observation to spot fish activity, coloured water, bubbles, weeds moving and so on. Carry some floaters with you and throw them into likely looking spots.

Try a quick cast

When you've found a swim you like, set up well back from the bank and try a quick cast close in. You can often get a fish. But banging in bivvy pegs, bank sticks, and splashing around in the water clearing reeds will send a fish far away.

Even then, don't pile in the feed if it's a new water or a new swim. Work the area carefully with a weight to find out what the bottom's like, where weed is heaviest, where there's gravel, and where there's clay, and so on. Time spent doing this is time well spent. If you don't, you could be casting to a barren area while a shorter or longer cast, or fishing to the left or right, might have put you on a hotspot.

Quick tip

GETTING THE CURVE RIGHT
Using a stiff curved link that won't curve the way you want? Just put it in a hot cup of water, set it the way you want then drop it into the water in front of you.

Top 9

fish that with just an extra 1 oz, you could be a record-holder
(fish on the IGFA list weighing just 1 lb)

1 Ozark Bass

2 Pinktail Chalceus

3 Sailor's Choice

4 Matrincha

5 Oniokoze

6 Grass Pickerel

7 Pluma Porgy

8 Panther Puffer

9 Blackline Tilefish

Feed their confidence

An hour spent feeding rather than fishing can result in confident fish. Fish too soon, and you can spook them. There will always be mug fish that take almost as soon as your bait hits the water, but if you want to catch a few, let them settle on the feed and get up their confidence. There are plenty of other tasks you can do: setting up a bivvy properly, brewing up, sharpening hooks, putting on new line and so on that will make the time pass quickly.

RING THE CHANGES
Try using a ring rather than shrink tubing on your hook. It gives more flexibility and is free to move and pivot, resulting in more hook-ups.

Long and the short of it

Use short hairs on pop-ups, longer hairs on bottom rigs.

Using PVA

Expensive PVA bags aren't always the best. Some rip as you cast, spraying boilies and pellets all over the place. Remember that particles must be dry when you put them in. Don't overfill or you won't be able to close the bag. About a third-full is ideal. Carry a variety of PVA: mesh, string, and tape. I prefer the latter as it's less likely to slip. Make sure that the rig cannot get tangled in the bag. Puncture the bag with a baiting needle to make sure it sinks when it hits the water.

Marmite might work

Looking for a different additive when temperatures are low?
Try Marmite or Vegemite. Another underused additive is salt.

Stonze for wary fish

Where fish have become very wary, camouflage your weights or
use Stonze. These are also very good for barbel, which seem to
sense a lead weight but can be fooled by Stonze, because they
are natural.

The best tigers

Using tiger nuts? I found some wonderful ones that had a
distinctive taste, and was told they came from Valencia, which
supposedly produces the world's best. They taste so good it's
easy to eat them yourself.

Get your boilies made

Making boilies can be time-consuming and make a terrible mess
of a kitchen. If you're using food colouring, leaving red stains
on a worktop will score zero domestic points. Save yourself the
trouble and use **www.boiliefactory.co.uk**. It will make boilies to
the flavour of your choice, and it's not expensive.

Clean it up

Finished fishing? Clear up after you. That includes not just paper,
tins, and bags but cigarette butts too. It's totally unacceptable
to shove litter underneath a bush. That's the way clubs and
syndicates lose waters. Don't throw all your unused bait in the
water, either. Take it home and refreeze it, or dump it in a dustbin.

Life at the bottom

Learn what it's like on the bottom, especially when you're fishing a new water. Just using the chuck-and-chance approach is a surefire way to increase your chances of a blank. Even the way that a lead lands can give you a powerful clue. Use braid, which is hyper-sensitive, and you will feel a thump as the lead hits bottom on a gravely or stony bottom. If there is little or no sensation, you're fishing over mud or in weed. Searching your swim like this can give you a very accurate picture, not just of depths, but also of how the bottom varies. If you're fishing over a gravely or stony bottom, it pays to check your hookpoint regularly. It's surprising how quickly even modern ultra-sharp hooks can blunt.

Try the no-weight route

Don't follow the crowd and automatically put on a 3oz lead so you can cast to the horizon. There will certainly be times when this is the best method, but you can often be king of the lake by using no weight at all. Carp learn quickly that weight equals danger, so freelining provides no resistance to a taking fish. You'll often find that the fish are hooked further back in the mouth because they take with more confidence.

Watch fish on a commercial fishery. When the anglers leave for their tea, that's when the carp come grubbing around the margins. You will often catch very big fish no more than a rod-length of line out, as long as you are quiet and cautious.

Try avoiding the hotspots

Hot pegs are often the ones near the car park, but there are many others that everyone makes for. You can tell them by the fact that there always seems to be someone fishing in that spot, and the grass will be very worn down. I suspect that if you carried out a survey, you would find most anglers head for the swims that look comfortable: easy to set up a bivvy, no trees to impede casting and a few features that look as if they will hold fish. Think about it: if there are only six people fishing a lake, and they always head for the same six swims, is it any surprise that those swims are the ones that produce the fish? Sure, there may be other reasons that the fish don't show so much in the 'unpopular' areas, but targeting these can sometimes pay dividends because the fish are often less cautious.

Quick tip

WARNING TO CLIMBERS
It's very trendy to climb trees to spot feeding fish. Certainly, a high vantage point can enable you to see things that are not evident at ground level, but a word of caution here. I have a friend who broke his leg in two places after falling out of a tree while carp-spotting. It may be fine in the film A Passion for Angling, where Chris Yates and Bob James leapt from a tree into the water at Redmire, and fun if you know what's below and don't mind getting wet; but if you're alone, falling out of a tree and getting injured could be very dangerous. If you're going to climb, check every branch you're planning to stand on.

Learn to swim

It's also tempting to use a boat, where allowed, for baiting up and fish-spotting. I'm amazed at the number of anglers who do so yet can't swim. If you can't, or you're a weak swimmer, wear a life-jacket. Boats can tip very easily when two people peer over the side at the same time, and the shock of cold water, plus heavy clothing, could kill you. You don't need to look like the Michelin Man: there are some terrific lightweight lifejackets, and even waistcoats that inflate on contact with water.

Beware of snagged braid

If you're caught in a tree or on the bottom, be very careful about pulling for a break. Even the popular way of wrapping line around your body and walking backwards can be very dangerous, especially if you're using strong braid. A 3 oz lead hurtling out of the water could easily kill you. There are various ways of freeing a snagged lead, the best one being to try another angle to free it. It's better to lose a lead than your eye. Never grab the line by hand and pull it across your face.

Quick tip

THROW THEM AWAY

Baiting up with boilies at range? If you don't want to disturb the swim with a spod, and if bait boats aren't allowed, then use a throwing stick. You'll be amazed just how far out, and accurately, you can send boilies.

An accuracy marker

If you're not sure that you're casting into the same spot, especially when spodding, you need to set a marker on your line. There's no point in identifying a feature if you're not going to fish accurately to it. Many people use slip knots, power braid or pole elastic, but I find that electrical tape is just as good because it won't slip. It's very cheap (a £1 roll will last you several seasons), it works with mono or braid and it can be easily removed without damaging the line in any way.

Cut off a 2.5 cm (1 in) section and pinch the line right in the middle. After sticking the tape to itself, trim it with fine, sharp scissors so that it is about 3 mm wide, and trim the front edge (careful you don't damage your line) so that it doesn't impede casting.

Foam will protect your hook

If you find your hook gets covered with debris on the bottom, or your bait twists back over the hook, use a small piece of hook foam. This slowly dissolves and when it comes clear, it will also show you where your bait is, enabling you to feed floaters accurately too.

Small is beautiful in winter

Scale down to catch in the winter. You can still tempt big fish by scaling down as small as size 12 hooks and 6 mm baits. Weed will be far less of a problem and even a 6 lb line will slice through what remains of most summer growth.

In 2005, golf professional Gary Hagues landed an 83 lb 8 oz world-record mirror carp from France's Rainbow Lake. The fish was weighed, tagged and he released it. He returned to Rainbow Lake in 2006 to enjoy the free vacation he won for catching the first carp and against all odds, on November 30th, 2006, he caught the same fish again to set another world record! This time the monster carp had reached 87 lb 2 oz.

TRICK THEM WITH TIPP-EX

If you find carp seem wary of your floater baits, try painting the hook with Tipp-Ex correction fluid (though don't paint the point) to make it less visible to fish coming up below the bait. For bottom fishing, you can now buy camouflaged hooks.

Patience will catch you more

Don't cast out and feed floating baits, but feed first and get the fish feeding confidently. Wait until at least a couple of carp are feeding and competing for the bait. Don't cast straight into the baited area, either. Cast beyond it and draw your bait or controller back slowly into the feeding area. You can often take more than one fish from a shoal if you cast to the periphery of where they are feeding, rather than right in the middle.

Use a floating line for this sort of fishing. Even then, it's worth treating it with floatant (Fox makes a good one) but don't put floatant right up to the hook: leave a few inches untreated.

Save at the supermarket

On a tight budget? You don't need to buy expensive colourings at your tackle shop. Supermarkets sell flavourings and colourings far more cheaply. You will also find that enhancing something like sausage meat with curry powder or spices can prove remarkably effective. Fish can become so wary of sophisticated baits that they can often fall for the simple approach.

The fishing was good;
it was the catching
that was bad.

A. K. Best

Competition fishing

chapter 3
Competition fishing

Wash your worms

Using chopped worm? Use a maggot riddle to take off the soil, then wash the worms in the water of lake or river you're fishing to clean them up. You can now chop them and you'll have pure worm. Mixing some chopped caster will enhance the mix, and adding concentrated worm juice will often work. But there's nothing better than the worms themselves!

You'll probably be using dendrobenas, which are easiest to obtain, but mixing a couple of lobworms is a good idea because a piece of lob often brings a big perch or large roach. Chop worms finely for silver fish; use bigger pieces for carp or when targeting big perch or bream. Pole pots are good to use as receptacles for chopping because there are no corners and it stops you doing too many worms at once.

Quick tip

GO SOFT ON SKIMMERS
Do you find that skimmers keep coming off? They have soft mouths and hooks pull out easily. You can try a smaller hook, but if you're on the pole, the answer is almost certainly to use softer (less strong) elastic.

Add line when it's shallow

In shallow water, especially on canals, the pole over their heads can scare fish. A waggler may not be as fast but if you can get presentation right, you might hold fish longer. Otherwise, try increasing the length of line between float and pole tip. It makes presentation harder and you may miss a few bites, especially in wind, but it's less likely to scare fish.

Don't mix jokers and maggots

Don't store jokers next to maggots; the ammonia from maggots seems to kill jokers. To keep jokers longer, give them a 'drink' each day. If you live in an area where the tapwater is heavily treated with fluoride, you might find rainwater is better. Keep a butt that takes overflow from your gutters. Once the jokers have had their daily drink, riddle them off and put them back in clean newspaper. Store the packs in the fridge. It's often worth splitting them into two; for some reason, they seem to store better. The best way of all to keep jokers in an aerated fish tank (don't put any fish in it!) and change the water every few days.

Get on the bomb

When you can't present a bait properly on the pole because of strong winds, put the pole down and switch to the lead. All too many anglers struggle on the pole when fishing a bomb or a waggler would be more effective. This is especially true if you're fishing long (14 m/45 ft or more) and it means you can explore more of the peg while giving your back a rest!

Olivettes can outfish shot

Many anglers prefer olivettes to shot. It's more aerodynamic and causes less twist on the strike. You can also concentrate more weight in an olivette: ideal if you're using a big flat float or catching fast with gudgeon or other fish close to the bottom

Quick tip

TREAT YOUR LINE

Fishing a waggler or stick float? Use a floating line spray for a stick float. On lakes and canals, you may want to sink your line. You can buy a special spray but diluted washing-up liquid works just as well.

Double up

Single maggot is a very effective bait, but you'll often pick up bigger fish with a double. Use three or four maggots on fast water, or where you're catching lots of fish. You can often get several fish without changing your bait. On such occasions, use an artificial maggot among the real ones to save time.

Feeding and boats

On a canal, feed after a boat has passed. The boat's undertow will often wash your feed out of the swim and topping-up means that there's something for fish to get their heads down on. Always look up and down the canal before feeding. You may find another boat is on the way!

Take the round route

A round mixing bowl is better than a square one. But it pays to run all your mixed groundbait through a riddle once you've kneaded it to take lumps out and to make sure it's evenly mixed.

Give them variety with paste

Carp fishing? Trying taking along two pastes: one hard, one soft. The harder, mixed the night before, is better when you've got to wait a while for bites, in deeper water, when there's a big undertow, or if you're being pestered by small roach. Mix your soft bait on the day. Whichever mix you use, keep it in polythene bags (split into two or three smaller helpings) to stop it drying out. Hemp and paste is a great and underused combination.

The stabiliser

Try leadcore line between your rig and elastic. It gives great stability.

Backing off the feed

Seems like bream have gone off feed? Take off that feeder and use a bomb over the same area. Often they're wary of the feeder.

Quick tip

A MOUSE CAN LOSE YOU A MATCH
Check your keepnets, especially if you haven't been out for a few weeks. A hungry mouse could lose you a match. Always carry a spare in your car.

Try colouring punched bread

Want to use punched bread? Take off crusts and flatten each slice with a rolling pin. Slice it into quarters, seal in airtight bags and use a little at a time. It's amazing how trying a fresh slice will ring fish when it appears that the swim has died. Carry a range of punch sizes. Sometimes a big bait will work, sometimes a small one. Try colouring a few slices with food dye, but wear rubber gloves unless you want green or red hands.

More is not always best

Most matchmen have caught on to additives. But if you're experimenting with carp additives, don't exceed the recommended doses. Using too much can repel rather than attract fish. Try these: geranium for winter roach, black pepper if you're fishing with meat, aniseed if you're on hemp and tares.

Backshot a stick

Fishing a stick float? I always use a backshot. It gives better control. If the wind comes up, don't be frightened of using two backshot and going as large as a No.1. Backshotting on the pole will give you precise control on windy days too.

Try the margins

On carp waters, the fish have learnt that anglers tip their bait in when they've finished. That's why you should always feed the margins, and try them late in the day, especially if you've got a feature like a tree or weed bed.

"Three-quarters of the Earth's surface is water, and one-quarter is land. It is quite clear that the good Lord intended us to spend three times the amount of time fishing as mowing the lawn.

Chuck Clark

The no-feed way

It's amazing how often you can pick up bonus fish in winter by not feeding at all, but simply casting a bomb into the right area.

Rotate your swims

Don't rely on one swim to produce all day. Close in and extreme range may provide you with bonus fish towards the end of a match, so feed these lightly and steadily. But feeding as many as five swims and rotating them can keep fish coming all day. Towards the end of the match, margins or the far bank of a canal, up the shelf, will often yield the biggest fish. Scale up if you think there's a chance of a big fish, rather than hoping you'll get it in on the rig that's been fine for small fish.

Try a tyer

Learn to use a hook tyer. They are more reliable and quicker. But it's always best to have several ready-tied hooks of the sizes you're likely to use. Add a dab of superglue for extra security. It's also useful to stop maggots 'blowing' up the line if you're catching a lot of small silver fish.

Shades of casters

Keep a range of caster colours. A change will often bring a fish. The lighter the caster, the quicker it will sink.

Beaten before you start

Don't be intimidated by having a renowned angler on the peg next to you. Fish your own match, especially if you know the water. Copying someone else rarely pays off.

Micro-swivels can cut tangles

If your hook lengths seem to tangle a lot, try using micro-swivels. You will also find that different-sized shot can be the culprit, even if they are all supposed to be No.4s or No.6s. When you put the shot on, line up the slits. Using double maggot or caster often causes frequent tangling, especially in windy conditions. Hook maggots or casters at different ends of the bait and they will spin less on retrieve. Don't fish on when your rig keeps twisting. Tie on a new hook length.

Quick tip

DOUBLE UP TO KEEP FISHING

Don't think: "It'll be all right on the day." Tie at least one duplicate rig of every tackle you're likely to use, and check that the float weight is what it says on the side. (It rarely is.) Little things like this mean your bait is out of the water less, meaning more chance of catching.

Colour-code your poles

Not sure what elastic you're using on each rig? Tie a spider knot and use different-coloured elastic bands to remind you. Equally, if you're using an external bung, buy different colours. Use an internal bung for thin or hollow elastics, otherwise an external one.

Fact

There is a simple method for accurately measuring a fish's swimming speed. When a fish is hooked and it makes a run, you measure how much line the fish takes off the spool in a certain number of seconds, and you can calculate the speed.

fantastic

Bream love fishmeal

Use a fishmeal-based groundbait if you're after bream. But it works less well for roach. Fishmeal groundbaits seem to attract larger fish, especially when you're after bream.

The night before

Soften pellets with bait pump, or soak them overnight. Put them in a bag, add flavouring, and close up. They need several hours for flavourings to soak in properly. It's not a morning-of-the-match job.

Making a noise

Commercial waters have given the lie to the old adage about keeping quiet. Making noise is often a real advantage. Use bagging wagglers that make a big splash as they hit the water. If loose-feeding, throw your bait high. Lift your float and let it make a noise, rather than lowering it gently. Even splashing the pole tip on the surface can encourage hungry carp. A good general tip is: cup if it's hard, ball if it's easy.

Off the top

Carp will feed very shallow. Once we thought 60 cm (2 ft) was shallow; now anglers are catching them at 10 cm (4 in). But you need specialist rigs to avoid tangles.

Droppers for accuracy

On running water, especially in winter, a bait-dropper can be a real boon for precise feeding and to keep your bait in the swim.

Meat tricks

If you're using a meat cutter, or even if you're slicing up meat, cut up some bits in smaller or larger lumps. Try breaking off pieces rather than using neatly cut squares. On heavily fished waters, the fish seem to learn that the squares can mean danger. Using a paste slop with hooked meat is often very effective. Another trick is to use two or even three pieces on the hook. Let meat sink naturally. You will often get bites on the drop.

Dig yourself in

Carry a small trowel. When fishing anything other than concreted swims, it enables you to do a bit of gardening and level off where your seat box and bait boxes go. There's nothing worse than your maggots tipping into the water on a sloping bank – except tipping in yourself. Another useful device that can prove a real boon is a weed-cutter. Use it to slice off overhead tree branches, position your keepnet among weeds or to clear a path between reeds.

Watch for cyclists

On canals, put your rollers along the bank, rather than behind you, if possible. There's less chance of clumsy walkers or cyclists running over your pole and smashing it.

Putting them back

Don't just tip up the bottom of the net to release your catch. Hold the net underwater and concertina the sections from the bottom upwards.

Frozen is good

Depressed because you've drawn a peg that's frozen over? Smash the ice, and you'll probably have a better day's sport than the anglers with open water. But watch out for the ice drifting back.

Clean your pole

Don't forget to clean your pole regularly. Attach a diamond-eye threader with a small piece of cloth attached (the stuff used for glasses is good). Dampen with warm water and keep pulling through until it's clean. Use this as a chance to check each joint and make sure there are no cracks. You can buy a repair kit that will fix small cracks. Keeping joints clean also means there's less chance of them sticking when you're trying to break down the pole. Use bungs for the break-down sections to stop grit entering the pole.

Don't pull back

Never pull a snagged rig directly back at you. Either do it underwater, or use a cigarette attached to a spare rig to burn off the line as close to the hook as possible. But try to avoid leaving lengths of line in trees because they can kill birds.

Quick tip

PEG IT OUT
Always peg out your net firmly on canals and rivers. There's nothing worse than having your net swept in by a fast-moving boat when it contains a match-winning catch.

"There's a fine line between fishing and just standing on the shore like an idiot.

Steven Wright

The world's largest fly-fishing rod and reel was completed on June 12th 1999 by Tiney Mitchell of Port Isabel, Texas, USA. The rod is an incredible 71 feet 4½ inches long and the reel measures 4 feet in diameter and 10 inches in width.

Corn on the drop

Fishing corn on the drop? It's a bait that sinks quickly. Try squeezing out some of the kernel before casting. This will make your hookbait sink slower.

Keep worms as pets

Keep a wormery. Every fish will eat worms, and it can be very expensive to keep buying worms. A healthy wormery will keep you supplied with a good stock all year. Add your vegetable scraps, grass, leaves and so on, and make sure you add water in dry times. You will find that it soon produces a rich store of redworms, which generally work better than dendrobenas, anyway. Just tip them back when you get home.

For some reason, lobworms don't do well in a wormery. You can keep them separately for some weeks in a large tub, but check it regularly and throw away any dead or cut worms, because they will kill off the rest. It's a good idea to build up a stock when it's damp, by going onto the lawn at night. If you don't have a garden, local parks are good but be prepared for wailing police sirens! Use a head torch, which leaves your hands free, and a worm container made of cotton with a drawstring, which can fit on a belt. A strong torch is not a good idea. The worms shoot back in their holes too quickly. A piece of white muslin or cotton over the glass will give a dimmer light. Lobs are a brilliant bait for bonus fish, especially perch, but they will produce specimens of most species. You'll get better results with a worm broken into halves or even sections, rather than a whole worm, because the juice seeps out and draws fish to it.

Let us spray

Buy an atomiser from a nursery or garden centre. They are very cheap, but are invaluable for keeping jokers fresh or for stopping groundbait from drying out. Use water from the lake, canal or river you're fishing in it.

Squatts are not just for bream

Squatts are more commonly known in some quarters as feeders and they are the larvae of the housefly. They are a brilliant attractor for bream, but they also work well for tench because they are a weak maggot and can't burrow as efficiently as a big maggot or a pinkie. They are regularly used on canals as hookbait for small fish where bloodworm and joker are banned, but they will also make a good hookbait for bream and tench. Fish 3 or 4 on a size 18 hook.

Change your pellets

Expander pellets have a low fishmeal content, so adding flavouring to them will enhance their appeal. Scopex and Tutti Frutti seem to work well. In cold weather, avoid using oil-based dips or high-powered oils. Oils float off a bait. This might work well in summer but just doesn't hack it in winter. Use water-based flavours instead.

Light and dark

Not sure about pellet content? Generally, darker-coloured pellets have a higher fishmeal and oil content, and work best in warmer weather. Use the lighter coloured ones when it gets cold.

Get on line

Unless you want to feed everyone else's swim, you must learn to cast accurately. Pick a marker on the far bank (one that's not going to move!) and aim for that. In deep water, don't flick over the bail arm straight away. It will mean that you may be fishing several feed short of where you thought. Only close the bail arm when you feel the lead or feeder hit bottom.

Remember the stretch

If you clip up with a light bomb but intend to use a feeder, remember that with mono, you must take account for stretch in the line. If you don't, you might find yourself casting into a tree. A good tip is to cast slightly short with a bomb to get the range, then clip up. Sometimes you don't want your bait to pour out of a maggot feeder; wind some duct tape around most of the holes. It's easily removed.

Beating the wind on the pole

In windy conditions, you will find that a bump bar will help you keep your pole still and improve presentation.

Minutes mean money

Save yourself time and catch extra fish by ensuring that
everything is within each reach. All too many matchmen bend
down every time they bait up. Set up trays at hand height so
that a slight movement puts you into your bait. Your keepnet
should, where possible, be right in front of you so that if a fish
falls off, it's going to fall into the net. A larger first ring can
save a few fish here. Ensure your handing net is within easy
grasp of your netting hand: if you hold the rod with your right
hand, the net should be on the left-hand side.

Keep other things that you might need like shot, a disgorger,
float caps, worm scissors and plummet on a bait tray rather
than buried in your tackle box. Even things like a drink
shouldn't mean you have to get up to find it. A few minutes
extra preparation can make all the difference during a match.
If it means you get in another dozen casts, one of those might
produce the bonus fish that wins you the match.

Watch out for jumpers

Some fish will jump out of a keepnet if you're not careful. Chub are the most notorious for this, but other species such as dace, trout, grayling, and carp will do so too. This can be a particular problem if you're river fishing on a fast-flowing swim, where the net mouth is close to the surface. To stop this happening, many anglers place their landing net over the net's open mouth.

But make sure that the net itself is securely lodged. On a gravely or rocky bottom, it's easy for your net to slip infinitesimally, and suddenly finish level with the surface. Modern tackle boxes have a keepnet attachment that makes this less of a problem. It might be a hassle to set up, especially if you've arrived at your swim late, but losing a 1 kg (2 lb) chub will soon make you realise that it was worth spending an extra minute or two making sure the net was fixed firmly.

Travelling with a trolley

Some venues demand route marches to reach your peg. On one Thames match, I had to walk more than 3 km (2 miles) in unrelenting sunshine. At times like that, you'll be glad you packed a trolley. If you've only got a short walk you won't need it, but if you face a long trek, you'll be very glad of it. Keep two spare bungee straps in your car or tackle box. You'll be astonished how they seem to disappear (probably nicked by your mates) and there's nothing worse than seeing your tackle roll off the box. Well, there is – when it falls off and rolls into the water. Always secure your tackle with more straps than you think you'll need.

If fishing is like religion, then fly-fishing is high church.

Tom Brokaw

Fly-fishing

chapter 4
Fly-fishing

Be a southpaw

Once you have learnt the basic overhead cast, try the same cast with your opposite hand. This can be very useful if there are trees or obstructions on one side. It's worth the effort to master more than the basic cast: a roll cast is important when there are trees or vegetation behind you. Again, try to perform this with either hand. Learn to sidecast. This is very useful when vegetation impedes a standard overhead cast.

Many anglers think that the Spey cast and Double Spey are too difficult. You can actually use both for trout fishing, and once you have mastered the basic principles of fly-casting (using the rod and the line's weight rather than raw muscle) you'll be surprised how easy these so-called advanced casts are.

Small is best

Large-diameter mesh will damage fish that are going to be returned. If your landing net mesh still has Queen Victoria's head on it, throw it away and buy a new small-mesh net. The small-mesh nets are also far less likely to snag your hook, and a tear in a large-mesh net can spell disaster if you net a fish and it slips through the hole while still hooked. A small tear in a small-mesh net won't cause the same problem (though get it fixed before you go fishing again).

A natural dry fly

Fishing the dry fly? If fish seem to be inspecting your fly and turning away, try this trick. Place a tiny split shot (between No.8 and No.12) on the leader 7.5-15 cm (3-6 in) from the fly. This will sink the key part of the leader just under the surface, but won't drag the fly itself below the surface film. It will, however, sink your fly just the slightest bit, making it ride less proud on the surface and look more natural.

Boat courtesy

You should also not cut into another boat's drift, or run your drift right on the line that they are fishing. When you work the same drift, don't motor straight through it. Sound magnifies, so move quietly in a boat. Banging on the side of a boat with a pipe, stomping around or shouting across to your mates can all make trout wary.

Sitting comfortably?

If you're boat-fishing, don't assume that you will be enjoying armchair-like comfort. Sitting on hard boards all day can leave you feeling as if you've had an operation for piles. Take your own cushion (a pillow in a waterproof bag is a good bet) or buy a proper boat seat. It will be one of your best investments, because you can't concentrate properly if you're uncomfortable and constantly shifting around.

Remember the bankers

When you're boat fishing, you have the opportunity to cover far more water than the bank anglers, so be polite and don't drift right through where they are fishing. Stay away from them. It's just basic angling courtesy.

A tip for life

Always wear a life jacket if you're boat fishing. You may be the world's best swimmer, but you won't get the chance to show it if you're burdened down in one-piece waterproofs. You don't need a bulky jacket; there are now some excellent lightweight ones that you won't even realise you're wearing.

Quick tip

STAY WARM

Carry an extra jumper or even better, a lined jacket, even when you're boat-fishing on a warm summer's day. It's surprising how much colder it can be out on the water, and when the sun starts to go down, which is usually the best time to fish, you want to be concentrating, not shivering. You can also use that extra jacket as a cushion.

On a big reservoir, you don't want to have to head back to the car park and pick up a warm coat when the fish are feeding.

Let technology help

Echo-sounders are now very cheap and can be a real boon if you're boat-fishing a large water. Not only does it identify the depths and where there are drop-offs or shallows, but it can show you barren areas and where there are concentrations of fish. It will also show you the depths at which fish are holding, making it easy for you to decide whether you should be using a floating line, an intermediate, or a sinker.

Increasingly on big waters, boat anglers are carrying hand-held GPS systems. With these, type in the coordinates to the memory, so you can head for 'hot' areas and land right on them, rather than drifting around, knowing it's somewhere around here. Another very valuable aid (and not just to boat anglers) is a thermometer. Changes in temperature have a very significant effect on the way fish feed. The changes will be most noticeable in shallow areas, where sunlight will warm these areas quickly. Equally, a cold wind will chill these areas faster than other parts of a lake or reservoir. Fish sense these changes much faster than we do. It may still seem quite warm, but the tour might already have moved to deeper areas.

Don't just dip the thermometer in the water and assume that's the water temperature. It will differ greatly, depending on the depth you're feeding. Use one with a split-ring in the top so you can explore the temperatures at different depths.

Top 5

anglers who hold all the fly-caught world records for one species

1 Herbert Ratner junior
(rock bass)

2 George P Mann
(brown bullhead)

3 Mary Filiault
(Pacific sierra mackerel)

4 Bud Korteweg
(double-spotted queenfish)

5 Margot Vincent
(Atlantic sailfish)

Tying in the dark

As the light starts to dim, tying a fly becomes much harder. I once wasted ages when trout were feeding at dusk trying to tie a fly, only to find when I returned to the car that I'd been trying to tie a fly that had the eye varnished over. You can carry a torch, but not many of us remember, and then you've lost your night vision just when you need it most. Try holding the fly up against the sky. It is one of the last things to go dark if it is not a cloudy day. Even then you can usually find a cloud big enough to use as a solid colour. Even a handkerchief held against the fly will make tying easier.

Pike on the fly

If you're fly-fishing for pike, look for the drop-offs. This is where pike like to lurk. You don't need a deep-sinking line to fish 6 m (20 ft) of water, either. Pike will come up several feet to attack a lure.

Most anglers pike-fish with flies that are far too small. Over the past year, I've been catching pike as small as 1 kg (2 lb) on a fly that's 25 cm (10 in) long. A large fish is also far more noticeable, and big fish prefer a big meal, rather than lots of little ones. Perch, too, will attack a very large fly. Don't be scared to fish one of 15 cm (6 in) or more.

Light-skinned damsels

Damsel nymphs are pale straw colour in the spring, and get darker as year progresses. If you're going to imitate what fish are feeding on, it makes sense first and foremost to get the colour right.

WATCH THE WEATHER

Check the forecast before you set out. Of course, this will tell you if it's going to teem with rain later in the day, so you know that you need to pack rainproof gear. But it will also tell you if the wind is going to switch round. On a heavily fished reservoir, for example, this will mean you can be in position before everyone else.

Casting in wind

Learning to cast when it's windy is an important skill, especially if you're paying a lot of money to fish somewhere like Argentina's Tierra del Fuego, where the wind never seems to stop blowing. Most anglers try to put more force into their cast to beat the wind. A sidecast can be effective, though it's less accurate, as it operates 60-90 cm (2-3 ft) above the water rather than 3.5-5.5 m (12-18 ft) above, where the wind is always stronger.

With a standard cast, when the wind is blowing into your face don't drive the rod tip further down to generate more energy and line speed. All you are doing is widening the casting arc. This produces a wider, open loop, which the wind will blow back into your face. Concentrate on a tighter loop, which will go through wind much more easily. Change the angle of your cast to open the loop just above the water, so the wind has less time to blow it off target. Rotating your arm slightly at the shoulder so your elbow moves back and up slightly will change the angle of your cast without affecting the casting arc.

Fly-fishing is the most fun you can have standing up.

Arnold Gingrich

Wade safely

Wading can be a nervy process on fast-flowing rivers. If you need to wade in rapid water to get to the other side, step downstream at an angle. It is much simpler and safer to wade downstream with the current than upstream against it – especially when the water is more than 60 cm (2 ft) deep. If necessary, get out of the water and walk upstream to a point that allows you to do so. The extra minute or two that it takes could save you getting wet. It could even save your life.

The clues in the river

Fishing a river with the wet fly and not sure what to put on? Spend a few minutes turning over stones. (A fine-mesh net such as those you can buy in pet shops is handy here.) It will give you a good indication of what the fish are finding themselves, and you've got a better chance of catching if your fly is similar to their natural food. If you're travelling light and looking to cover several miles during the day, check with your bug net every so often. It's surprising how much this can change over a few hundred yards.

Long and the short of it

Trout landing nets usually have short handles to make them easy to carry, but you'll find a long-handled landing net much better when boat-fishing. It also means you don't have to bring a fish right alongside the boat, which can be a little tricky with longer rods. Never chase a fish when it's ready to net. Bring the fish over the net. If you chase it, a late plunge can pull the line against the net frame and dislodge the hook.

Small can be beautiful

Many reservoirs stock with larger trout simply because of cormorants, which have a bit more trouble stuffing down a fish of this size. Doesn't mean they can't do it (I've seen pictures of cormorants with sea trout up to 2 kg/4 lb down their gullets) but the fish have a bit more chance. Very big trout (over 4½ kg/10 lb) that are stocked into small waters may look very impressive in a photograph and even be an ego trip for your phone or screensaver, but they are invariable short, ugly fish that don't fight like true wild trout, but wallow rather than pull. Catch one if you must to get it out of your system, but then start to appreciate the fun of smaller trout on lighter tackle.

Long ago, when dinosaurs roamed the land, trout did not start at 1 kg (2 lb). On the little rivers I fished, 200 g (8 oz) was a whopper. If you're fishing brooks and streams, appreciate the beauty of small trout and realise that the environment does not allow it to grow to 9 kg (20 lb). You can have terrific sport on small rivers and upland lakes that hold small, wild brown trout. Scale your tackle down. You don't need a 2¾ m (9 ft) liner and 3 m (10 ft) rod. Even a 1-weight or 2-weight will be heavy enough on little waters, where you can use a 1 kg (2 lb) cast and small flies.

Match the light

Wear clothing and a hat that blends into the background or sky. Don't silhouette yourself against the skyline. Trout don't have eyelids. Use bright sunlight to hide you if you can get it behind you without casting a shadow on the trout. 'Keep low, move slow' is good advice. You'll catch many more fish.

Buy a licence

Buy a fishing licence. Of course, you'll sometimes get away with it. But that money goes towards fishery work from which you're benefiting. Don't be a cheapskate! Getting caught can also land you with a big fine. The maximum fine in the UK is £2,500. You won't get hit with that, but it could easily be £400 plus costs. Makes the licence seem cheap, doesn't it? Remember that if you're fishing for salmon or sea trout, you will need a different (and more expensive) licence.

You don't need a £5,000 reel

You can pay up to £5,000 for a fly reel. You might want to impress your friends on the bank, but a reel is merely a line holder and for most fly-fishing (the tackle trade won't thank me for saying this) you can manage perfectly well with a cheap reel costing no more than £50. Cheaper reels generally offer spare spools free as well. Even if your reel does not offer this, get a couple. It means you can carry a floater, a sinker, and an intermediate, and change quickly depending on conditions.

Get trained

Having problems with your casting, or want to learn a new cast? Book a couple of lessons with an approved instructor. (You'll find their names at the back of most fly-fishing magazines.) Like golf lessons, you'll be surprised at the difference it can make, and as well as improving your casting, it will sort out any problems you might be having. If you find that your wrist or back ache after a day's fishing, it's time to book a lesson.

Auctions for cheap tackle

A brilliant place to buy decent fly reels cheaply is a specialist tackle auction. Most of the people there are collectors who are not interested in modern tackle. You can pick up some very good reels in near-mint condition for way under trade price, and they will often have line on them too. They are also a good place to buy modern carbon trout and salmon rods. Collectors only want split-cane! Classic tackle auctions are also wonderful places to buy fly-tying materials cheaply. You will sometimes pick up rare feathers that are no longer available, such as macaw. Your lines will cast better if you use a line cleaner regularly. These take off all the minute bits of dirt that accumulate on the line, slowing its progress through the rings.

A key lesson

It might seem very amusing to watch someone strip off and dive into a lake, trying to retrieve their car keys – until it happens to you. Put your keys on a floating keyholder so it can't happen. Don't think it won't happen: it's all too easy when you're searching through pockets for something for your keys to catch on your sleeve and flip out. It never happens in shallow water, either.

Fish in comfort

The fast-dry shirts made by companies like Ex Officio and Columbia are ideal for saltwater fly-fishing, because they protect your skin yet are very light. They are very comfortable and if it rains, they dry within minutes.

What you must wear

Always wear a hat and glasses when fly-fishing. Both will protect your eyes from the less than perfect cast, while a hat can stop you getting a flying hook in your head. A hat also keeps the sun off your face, and a large brim helps with spotting fish. If you're sight-hunting for fish, buy a good pair of Polaroids, and attach them with retainers. It's easy for a clumsy cast to flick them off. You will have your own favourite colour but I've found that an amber brown seems to give the best vision on all but those very bright days. Then I'll change to crimson or grey. The classic rule for salmon fishing is big flies for early season, smaller flies as the season progresses.

Quick tip

VARNISH THE BOBBIN-HOLDER
When tying flies, do you find that the bobbin holder sometimes cuts the thread? Then try this trick. Put a very thin layer of quick-drying varnish into the tube. This will harden and cover those abrasive edges.

Moving in the margins

Not sure where to fish at the start of the season? If you're in a boat, you will probably get better results by working the margins rather than the open water. This water, being shallower, warms more quickly. Early-season rainbows tend to shoal, especially stockies, so once you find the fish you should get plenty of takes. That's why it pays to keep moving.

WAIT UNTIL YOU WADE

If you're bank-fishing, don't wade in as far as you can go and start fishing. The smart angler sets up quietly and well back from the bank, and fishes the water in front of him before going anywhere near the water. Trout will hold in surprisingly shallow water – but not if you splash around in it.

Learning a new water

Fishing a new water? Remember that shoals of fish follow bank contours. Headlands are always a good place to try for ambushing fish as they move around a lake. Shallows, weed beds, scum mats and silty bottoms all mean places where trout food lives. Rocky shallows are good when the wind is blowing inshore because that's where trout will come hunting for food blown to them. Areas where shallows drop off into deeper water will be hotspots. As a general rule, save the deeper water for warmer parts of the season. When it gets very hot, look for places where there is some movement, either caused by the wind, or there may be an inlet or stream.

The well-worn spots aren't always the best. Often anglers choose these because there are no obstructions behind and casting is easy, or because they are a short walk from the car park! The best way to learn where to go on a new water, though, is to talk to the locals and the fishery manager. He wants you to catch fish, so you'll come back!

Fact

The world's most expensive lure is the Million Dollar Lure from MacDaddy Fishing Lures. This 12 inch trolling lure, designed to catch marlin, is made with over 3 lb of gold and platinum, and encrusted with 100 carats of diamonds and rubies. The price, as the name indicates, is $1 million.

fantastic

Top 5

line-class world records just waiting for a claim

1. Grayling (all records vacant)

2. Porbeagle Shark on 2lb line

3. Red Piranha on 4lb line

4. Wels on 8lb line

5. Zander on 12lb line

women's line-class world records just waiting for a claim

1. Bass on 6lb line

2. Bluefin Tuna on 4lb line

3. Conger on 6lb line

4. Halibut on 130lb line

5. Porbeagle Shark on 20lb line

Check for leaks

Before the season starts, check your waders. Fill them up in the bath and examine each section to see if there are bubbles coming up, which means you've got a leak. If you're going away, always carry a repair kit with you. There are some rivers (those in Russia, Mongolia, and Canada, for example) where it's impossible to fish without neoprenes. A leak and no repair kit means you'll just have to watch others catching fish.

Never wade further than you feel comfortable, even if a ghillie is encouraging you to go out farther. On some of the Scottish rivers, you should always carry a wading stick and move slowly. Thirty seconds won't make a lot of difference to the fish, but an unwary step could spoil your day. It could even drown you.

It's worth buying a special wading waistcoat which can take a lot of gear (spare flies, zinger, forceps, spools of line) to save you plodding back to the bank and disturbing the water every time you want to change something. There are also wading jackets that double as lifejackets, which are a sensible buy if you're an unsteady wader or you can't swim.

When wading, always wear a wading belt so the waders can't fill up with water. If you do lose your footing, don't panic. Drop your rod (you can always get another rod, but not another life) and try to get on to your back, paddling with your hands towards the bank.

Tape your rod

Unless you want to paddle up to your neck, always tape your rod sections together when fly-fishing. It's easy for them to work free, especially when Spey casting.

Big isn't always best

You would think that the longer the rod, the better it is for casting. But you'll find that a 2¾ m (9 ft) rod will give you far better accuracy than a 3 m (10 ft) one.

Dapping isn't just for Ireland

Dapping traditionally takes place on Irish loughs where there is a hatch of mayfly. But you don't need a mayfly hatch. You can use a live daddy-long-legs, grasshopper, even a blowfly. Check that your water allows it first, and use a long rod (telescopic rods of 5 m/16 ft or more are ideal). You need a length of floss, which you can buy in most good tackle shops, of about 3 m (10 ft), then a length of leader of 2-3 m (6-10 ft).

Use a fine-wire hook and use a couple of flies. Let the boat drift and keep your rod high, with the dapped insect just touching the water. Try not to let the floss go into the water. You need a decent wind, and you must not strike quickly. Wisdom says you should say something like God Save the Queen before striking (though the Irish have a slightly more trenchant expression) to stop you hitting the fish too early.

If you're dapping with mayfly, I've found that adding a daddy-long-legs to a couple of mayfly seems to bring bigger fish. I don't know why, but it works. Don't try catching 'daddies' with your hands. Take a large, fine-mesh net, and keep them in something like a four-pint plastic milk container. This makes them easy to get out but hard for them to escape.

Use rings to join

Use leader rings when joining lines of different strengths. You'll have fewer worries about your knot and get fewer tangles too.

Try an intermediate

For most summer and autumn salmon fishing, people use a floating line. But sometimes you'll find that switching to an intermediate will bring a take when it doesn't seem as if you're going to catch.

Learn from the ghillie

Listen to your ghillie (your well-versed attendant!) when salmon fishing – but don't be frightened to try something different, whatever they say. A successful fly is not always the best one, but if it's the fly that everyone is using, it's no surprise that the fish are being caught on it. On the other hand, a ghillie is going to get a better tip if you catch fish, so he's not going to put you on a loser.

Quick tip

A CLEAN KILL
Never leave a fish flapping around in the boat or in your fish bag. Either return it straight away (best to unhook in the water if you can) or dispatch it straight away with a priest (an elegant wooden or metal truncheon).

Your private boat

Some anglers are using belly boats to fly-fish for sea species. (I'm told it's great fun when you hook a tope.) But if you do so, make sure you have a companion and be very wary of rip currents. It's sensible to carry a couple of flares for an emergency.

If you're fishing from a belly boat on stillwaters (and you'll be surprised at the number of waters that allow it) make sure you have a good pair of neoprene waders, of at least 4 mm (1/8 in) thickness. Goretex waders might be less sweaty in warm conditions, but they seem to wear out quickly, with the rubbing wearing out the fabric behind your knees.

Belly boats are also great for pike fishing to access those areas that are impossible to reach from the bank and difficult from a boat. Always wear a lifejacket when belly-boating. I'd advise having the CO_2-powered ones. But if anglers are fishing from the bank, keep well away from them. It's very impolite to disturb their fish.

Quick tip

PUTTING FISH BACK

If you're returning salmon (and these days, it's generally the rule rather than the exception) do so quickly and don't leave it bouncing around on a rocky bank. If you want a picture, take it in the water and return the fish quickly. Hold it in the water, facing upstream, until it swims off by itself. As Lee Wulff said: "Salmon are far too valuable to be caught only once."

"There is no greater
fan of fly-fishing
than the worm!"

Patrick F. McManus

Cast from a tray

A line tray will protect your line and make casting far easier if you're shore fishing for trout: no loops of line to tread on and get caught around your body. But it's also an invaluable accessory when boat-fishing for pike and beach fishing for bass, mackerel, and pollack.

Big trout in the fall

Autumn is generally the best time to catch a very big trout. Look for shoals of fry and you will usually find the biggest trout. Use fry patterns, or marabou-tailed patterns fished a few feet below the surface on a jerky retrieve. As the water temperature drops, insect life starts to die off. That's the time to try a small dark nymph pattern, fished at depth, or a Hare's Ear on a sinking line fished with a slow retrieve.

Try the dry

Dry-fly fishing might have acquired an elitist tag but don't let that worry you. It's one of the nicest ways to catch fish, especially when you can see them. Water doesn't have to be crystal-clear to catch fish, and you don't need a hatch of flies to make it worth fishing. Fish are always on the look-out for a meal. When dry-fly fishing, don't cast directly at a fish. Aim to land your fly 60-90 cm (2-3 ft) upstream. If you can see a fish but it won't take, leave it alone and come back later.

Keeping the rings unfrozen

When it's very cold, you might find that the droplets of water on your line turn to ice and freeze up your top ring. Just put some Vaseline on the rings and you won't have the problem.

DULL WAY TO OUTSMART BIG FISH

You'll probably have a better chance of catching on heavily fished waters if you use a dull-coloured fly. Especially on waters holding big fish, you'll find that the trout have become very wary of gaudy flies, especially if they've been hooked.

Salmon on a dry fly

One of the most popular methods on Canadian rivers is salmon-fishing with a dry-fly called a Bomber. This is fished on a dead drift, though on many rivers salmon will take if the fly is skated across the top. A Bomber would certainly work if more anglers fished with it outside Canada.

Practise on coarse fish

Most species will take a fly, and practising on chub, dace, and carp is a great way of learning to present a fly properly and how to play fish on light leaders. Not every water holds trout, but almost every water holds coarse fish, so you can pop down your local river for an hour after work, and fishing is often free.

Indicators to spot small takes

Unless you've got excellent eyesight, you'll probably find that an indicator will help you spot takes when upstream nymphing, especially when using heavy Czech nymphs. Make sure indicators are allowed, though. Strike at the slightest movement.

Nymphing for salmon

Upstream nymphing can also work for salmon and sea trout, though we don't often have the river clarity that you get in places like New Zealand and Canada. If you are fishing to a salmon, twitch the fly as the nymph gets near the fish.

Learn to double-haul

When fishing for saltwater species like bonefish, you need to learn to double-haul and to cast accurately in wind. You'll enjoy the fishing more, catch more fish, and won't find your guide shouting at you quite as much!

Quick tip

POLE ELASTIC TO MAKE BLOODWORM
Pole anglers are helping the fly fisherman. The elastics that they use inside their poles to handle big fish make an excellent material for tying artificial bloodworm.

It's not always a sinker

Don't assume that you have to use sinking lines in the winter. With warmer temperatures now seemingly the norm in the darker months, you will often find fish in the top 2 m (6-7 ft), so try a floater with a single weighted pattern, especially on small waters. A floating line gives you more control of your fly to fish at different depths simply by varying the speed of retrieve.

Re-treat the leader

Using a sinking leader? Remember that the degreasing agent you use will wash off. You'll need to reapply it frequently, and that means a lot more often than every hour!

Uni-knot is best

Most anglers use a half-blood knot to tie their fly to a leader. Learn to tie a uni-knot. Tests show that it's far stronger (an average 90 per cent knot strength, compared to 60 per cent for the half-blood). You can also tie it so that it is not pulled tight to the eye of the hook. Leaving a small loop will give added movement to a fly.

Tipping your guide

Typically, you tip a ghillie 10 per cent of the day's fishing fee, perhaps a little more if he has clearly worked hard for you or you've been very successful. If you're not sure of the right amount, check in advance with someone who fishes the water regularly. If you're undertaking adventure fishing in a remote area such as India or Mongolia, be wary of overtipping. Giving too much may mean you won't see your guide next day!

I love fishing. It's like transcendental meditation with a punchline.

Billy Connolly

Sea fishing

chapter 5
Sea fishing

Put sharks back

Sharks have a bad reputation, but they provide terrific sport. You can get all the trophy you need with a photo, rather than killing such a fine fish. The porbeagle population has declined by 90 per cent since 1960s. Don't make the figure worse.

Estimating a tope's weight

Want to estimate a tope's weight? Here's the recognised way to do it without damaging the fish. You might need a calculator here, or just write the numbers down and do the maths when you get home. Measure the fish's girth (the distance around the deepest part of its belly) and multiply that by the same number. (So if the fish's girth is 25 in, multiply it x 25.) Now measure its total length to the fork of the tail and multiply that number (again in inches) by the figure you've got from multiplying the girth. Now divide that number by 800. So 25 x 25 = 625, x length (say, 42) = 26, 250 divided by 800 = 32.8125, or 32 lb and about 13 oz. It's not as hard as it sounds!

Unhooking doggies

Small dogfish may be a nuisance, but that's no reason to mistreat them. Put them back too. To unhook, bend the tail so you can hold it and the head at the same time.

Float-legering

When float-fishing from a pier or rocks, does your float drift out of the hot area too quickly? Then cast out a weight, tighten up, and connect your float rig with a double-ender. Slip it on to the line, raise your rod top and it will hold in position.

Mackerel killers

Only catch the number of mackerel you need. The belief that you can return them to the sea after catching isn't true. Simply touching them causes them to die. Mackerel have very thin skin which enables them to move very quickly through the water. Merely touching this damages it enough to ultimately kill them. I only found it out this year!

Take away your rubbish

Check that you've cleared out all your bait after a day's fishing. If you leave a mackerel or a pack of lugworms in your fishing bag and don't fish for a few weeks, the smell will haunt you for months. Take your litter home or put it in a rubbish bin – especially used line. This can trap birds' legs. With line, it's best to burn it. Don't leave crushed crabs, dead ragworm or cut up mackerel on a pier or rocks, and don't throw newspaper in to the sea. Some of the finest shore fishing is now out-of-bounds to anglers, simply because they have left such a mess in the past. Clear up your newspaper and bait after you.

Clean your reels

Always wash off your reels after fishing in the sea. Saltwater is very corrosive, and sand gets everywhere. Use warm water and leave them to soak for 10 minutes, then dry them lightly and let them dry off naturally.

Groundbaiting can work

Try groundbaiting for sea fish. It's easy for fish like mullet when you're fishing in a harbour or off rocks, but you can do it from a beach, pier, or even a boat. When there's little tide, using a freshwater swim-feeder filled with bits of ragworm, lugworm or crab can bring bites when it appears that nothing is feeding. Another good bet is to buy tins of cheap fish from a supermarket and mash it up. (This is best done on the shore or boat, rather than at home!) You can even use a weighted tin filled with bits of fish for tope or skate. Try using an additive such as those used by carp anglers. A lot of these are fish-based with flavours like crab or halibut. A bit of sponge soaked in an additive (dilute a little because the scent can actually be too strong) and put in to the swim-feeder is a great way of drawing fish to you.

Quick tip

TRY DIFFERENT-COLOURED FEATHERS
If you're using feathers, it pays to have them in different colours. Red feathers seem to bring better results in kelp, for example.

Tide tables are invaluable

Carry a tide table. It depends where you are fishing, but certain states of the tide will be the most productive. If you're short of bait (for example, you've only got a few peelers or a couple of live sandeel) it makes sense to put on your prime bait when there's the best chance of catching a fish.

The biggest bass

If you're fishing live mackerel for bass over a reef, the biggest fish is very often the first one to take the bait.

Rescuing a cancelled day

Fish like flounders and bass will come a long way up a river. Both are regularly caught from the Thames in the middle of London, for example. So if your favourite spot is too rough to fish, or your boat skipper won't go out because the forecast is poor, find a spot upriver and you'll be surprised what you can catch. You can also fish lighter, which makes bite detection easier.

Quick tip

PROTECT YOUR SKIN
It doesn't need blazing sun to cause sunburn. The reflection of the sun off the water can burn you badly on seemingly cloudless days. Rub on some sunscreen when you're boat fishing in the summer, and make sure you put some on your hands and your ears too.

The right rod

If someone has given you a beach-casting rod and it has only four or five rings, it's meant to be used with a fixed spool reel. If it has eight rings or more, it's meant to be used with a multiplier. It doesn't mean you can't use a multiplier on a fixed-spool rod and vice versa, but it won't cast as well and it will put unnecessary strain on the rod and line.

Join a casting club

If you're beach-fishing, be careful that swimmers or surfers are nowhere near when casting. A 170 g (6 oz) lead can kill. If you're a newcomer, go somewhere with lots of open space and practise your casting. Even better, join one of the casting clubs (fishing magazines will give their addresses) and learn properly.

Keeping sandeels alive

Sandeels are one of the very best baits but they are hard to keep alive. A charter boat that's fishing with sandeels should supply an aerated container, but if you're fishing inshore on your own boat, you can rig up a simple system. You need to keep constant aeration, though, and you must change the water regularly. The same applies if you're fishing live mackerel for big bass, tope, or shark. That said, sandeels are an excellent bait dead too, but cut off their tails, which impede casting and cause tangles. They are quite a soft bait so if you're distance casting, use tying elastic to hold them on.

Pump your bait

Digging your own bait? It can be tough work. Try using a bait pump for lugworm. It takes a bit of practice but saves you an aching back!

Watch out for weevers

If you're netting your own sandeels, only take what you need for bait (and perhaps some to freeze for future use). Be careful when you're sorting through a net for sandeels. Weevers, the only poisonous European fish, inhabit the same sandy ground and if you grab one accidentally, your day's fishing is over. It's very unlikely that a weever will kill you, but the poison in their dorsal fins is very painful. (I'm speaking from personal knowledge here!)

If you're unfortunate enough to get stung, pour vinegar over the puncture wound. Do this over a bowl so that you can keep reusing the vinegar. Doing this for a few minutes continuously will immobilise the stinging cells that have not yet penetrated. A paste of equal parts of baking powder (sodium bicarbonate) and water put directly on the punctured skin and surrounding area is said to draw out the poison.

Dust meat tenderiser around the affected area which will make any remaining cells stick together. (Many thanks to **www.worldseafishing.com** for this tip, though you'll probably have to find a supermarket as most anglers don't carry meat tenderiser, baking powder, and vinegar with them.) You should go to a hospital anyway.

Fact

Dr Martin Arostegui of Coral Gables, Florida, a retired physician, holds nearly 200 world records. For three years in a row (2005-2007) he broke more freshwater, fly, and saltwater records than anyone else in the world.

Try a bluey

A new bait, blueys, which are similar to sandeels, are producing excellent catches. You can only buy them frozen. Artificial sandeels have also improved from the days of the Eddystone Eel (though it's still a great bait). The soft rubber imitation eels are very effective and in a good tideflow, you can have almost as good results as with a live eel.

Double your chances

When fish are feeding, set up two rigs. Pre-bait one and clip the old one off and clip on the new one, then just cast out. The longer your bait is in the water when fish are feeding, the more chance you've got of catching fish!

Change with the tide

Don't blindly use the same lead whatever the state of the tide. A 170 g (6 oz) or heavier lead may be needed when the tide is pushing through, but a much lighter one (even as small as 28 g/ 1 oz) will give you better bait presentation. You can also use lighter lines to give better bite detection and, often, more bites.

Float fish around the piles

On piers, try float fishing when there isn't a lot of tide. You can hold the float around the piles of the pier, where bass, pollack, mackerel and scad will be hunting for small fish. A float enables you to present a bait well off the bottom more naturally. You don't always need the things like marker buoys that are often sold as 'sea floats' either. On many piers, I've fished with freshwater floats, using them sliding on the line.

A BLUNT LESSON

Always carry a sharpening stone with you. When you're fishing over rocky ground, or hooking fish with hard mouths like wrasse, modern needle-point hooks can blunt rapidly. Don't assume that because a hook is new, it's going to be sharp.

Always use a shock leader

If you're casting any distance, always use a shock leader. This will save you cracking off and losing leads; it also means that if you miscast, the lead won't come off and injure someone severely. Whether you're using a multiplier or a fixed spool, it's a good idea to use a thumb-guard for casting. Line cutting into your finger can be very painful!

Fishing on holiday

Wherever you go on holiday, you will almost always find some decent sea fishing. But don't leave it until you arrive to book a boat. A good skipper should be booked heavily for a couple of weeks. One who is always available will probably be of the variety who stops in a random piece of ocean, says: "This is a good spot" and goes to sleep. The internet is a great facility to check out the best boats from any port. Big-game boats can be very expensive, but once again, you can use the internet to find other anglers who might be going at the same time, and share a boat to cut costs.

"Even eminent accountants are known, in their capacity as fishermen, blissfully to ignore differences between seven and ten inches, half a pound and two pounds, three fish and a dozen fish.

William Sherwood Fox

Put billfish back, but…

These days, most billfish are returned. But in countries like The Gambia, where a fish is vital food for a village, you'll have to accept that everything you catch will be supper for someone. It's no use getting high and mighty about it. Don't fish if you don't like the idea.

The first lesson

The first tip I ever read about sea fishing was: never argue with your boatman about religion or politics. It's still good advice.

Brighter beads

Luminous floating beads can increase your catches in murky water.

Ease the tension

When you've arrived home and washed off your reels, loosen the drag on a multiplier reel before putting it away. This takes pressure off the clutch plates and prevents them from seizing. But don't loosen them right off because dirt and grease can get in. A tension of around 450 g (1 lb) is about right.

Attracting flatties

Fishing for flatfish? It's amazing how many more fish you'll catch using beads and moving the bait frequently. For flounders, a flounder spoon creates vibrations in the water and attracts fish. Flounders will come into very shallow water (I've caught them in just 15 cm/6 in) so it pays to wind in very slowly and keep stopping, especially when using crab as bait.

The best bait of all

Crab is, to my mind, the best of all sea baits. But it's extremely expensive to buy, so learn to collect your own. On less populated stretches put out old tyres (you'll need to attach them to something or they'll wash away) or large tins. If using rocks, put a smaller stone under the rock so a crab can creep beneath.

Always check beneath a hard-backed crab. It will protect a peeler or a softie, the latter by holding the vulnerable crab upside down, the former by covering it. Keep your crabs in damp seaweed and give them an occasional drink by covering them with seawater, leaving for a few minutes, then emptying the water out.

If you want peelers to get closer to the peeling stage, put them in sea water. Don't throw the legs and claws away; these can festoon a lump of crab and add attraction. You can also get a few more baits out of the crab. I like to cut a crab so the juices wash out. If you're casting from a pier or beach, use elastic to keep the crab on.

Low tide will give you clues

One of the best ways to decide where to fish from a beach or pier is to take a walk at low tide. It will show you features such as mussel beds, gullies, and snags that won't be apparent when the tide rises. A useful tip if you're fishing from a beach or pier where the tide goes out a fair way is to do a spot of bait-digging where you intend to fish. It's good exercise and it will often bring you bonus fish, especially if you leave bits of broken rag or lugworm among the digging.

If you're bait-digging, make sure that you don't need permission, and if you're digging close to a shore where people swim, tread down where you've dug. It can be very dangerous as the tide comes in.

Don't mix rags and lugs

Don't mix rag and lugworm in the same container, and as soon as you've finished digging, sort out the broken worms from the whole ones. The former will kill the whole worms.

Quick tip

BIG BAITS FOR COD
It's astounding how big a bait a small cod can take.
If you're using lugworm, using several worms will give you a far better scent trail. When fishing from a beach, don't worry if you're not much of a caster. Cod hunt closer to shore in the darkness.

Don't worry about casting short

Trying to cast 150 m (160 yd) can be counter-productive. Fish like flounders and bass can be caught very close to the beach, where they hunt small fish, crabs, and shellfish washed around by the tide. Fish hang around breakwaters, groynes, inlets, rubbish pipes and pontoons, so why cast away from them?

On piers, many anglers try to cast as far as they can, but your quarry is often right under your feet. A gentle lob out usually produces a lot more fish.

Snags mean fish

Fish like snags. They hang around kelp and rocks. You have to face the fact that you're going to lose some tackle in such spots. On snaggy ground, don't use grapnels. They will keep getting caught up.

Making your own leads cuts down on the cost, and using a 'rotten bottom' means you won't lose fish and lead. If you're fishing fairly close off rocks, or off a pier, attach the lead to a line that is at least 2 kg (5 lb) lighter than the main line. Don't try this if casting a long way because there is a danger of snapping off.

There are various rigs when using a rotten bottom and casting at distance, including modified leads and using a loop system with weaker line that will not break off on the cast but will break free when the lads hits the water. One of the simplest rotten bottom rigs is to use a paperclip as your connector.

Snip the squid

Congers and huss will often snip the head off when you're using whole squid as bait. So remove the head and bind the body to the hook.

Using braid

Braid line can be very effective for boat fishing because its thinner diameter means you can use much lighter weights. But use a glove when winding it onto your reel, and remember that braid has no stretch, so you don't need to strike; just wind into a fish. Striking, especially in shallow water, will probably lose you the fish.

Protect your eyes

Winding a swivel into your top eye can break it and severely weaken the link. The worst thing about damaging a rod eye is that you rarely notice it until the line suddenly snaps. First, check lined rings after every trip. Putting a couple of beads above the top swivel acts as a protector; use beads on either side of every swivel.

Fun with dropnets

Take a dropnet with you when fishing from a pier. If you catch a big fish, it means you've got a chance of landing it. Don't assume someone else on the pier is bound to have a net. Second, it can provide you with bonus bait such as whelks, hermit crabs, and prawns, and if you've been lumbered with looking after children, catching crabs will keep them happy for hours!

Unhooking the lippy ones

Some sea fish have very fleshy mouths that make removing a hook difficult. Carry a sea disgorger or a pair of pliers. (The latter is also useful for many other tasks, like tightening or loosening a nut on your reel.)

Avoid the spikes

Be careful of fish like bass, which have very sharp gill covers. Unless you're entirely confident about holding fish, use a damp towel. You will also need to watch for the sharp dorsals of most species, and the needlepoint spike on the side of fish like flounders.

Kill cleanly

If you're going to take a fish home to eat, kill it quickly and humanely. Don't leave it to die slowly. You can use a rock, but a weighted piece of wood, similar to that used by salmon anglers, is easier. You might prefer to clean your fish at sea, rather than when you get home. If you do so on a pier don't leave the rubbish lying around. Wrap in newspaper and put in a rubbish bin.

Catching prawns

Catching prawns is much easier at night. You need a fine-mesh net and a strong light. Ideally, it's best done in a harbour. Shine the light on the water and the prawns will be attracted to the light. You'll see their eyes shining. Just scoop 'em out. But keep them in water with some seaweed in it. If you're going to keep them alive for fishing the next day, the best bet is to put them in an aerated fish tank.

You can transport containers of seawater, but a far better idea is to buy some sea salt at a specialist aquarium shop selling saltwater tropicals. Follow the instructions on the bag of salt. You'll need to set your tank up a few weeks beforehand. Out of season, it's fun to catch some gobies or tiny flatfish and keep them in the tank, especially if you use different coloured sands with the flatfish, because they will change colour to match the habitat. A fish tank is good for storing any sort of seabait, but be careful what you mix in it. Putting crab and ragworm in the same tank, for example, is not a good idea...

Prawns are a great bait fished live, but you can still catch well on dead prawns. Shrimps are another good and underused bait for flatfish.

Don't get cold

The forecast might be blazing sun, but the weather can change rapidly on the coast. Always carry a totally waterproof outer garment and clothing that will keep you warm, especially if you're night-fishing. It's a good idea to have a spare set of clothing in your car because a rogue wave can soak you, and leave you shivering in wet clothing. Always carry a hat. Woolly hats may not look elegant, but they'll keep your head warm. The body loses much of its heat from the head.

Revenge on bait-stealers

If you're being pestered by very small fish such as pouting, whiting or smelt, try using them for bait. This can often bring you a big cod from a boat, or bass from a pier.

Quick tip

SHARP KNIVES ARE SAFER
Sharpen your baiting knife before every trip. It's actually safer to have a sharp knife than a blunt one.

Keep your feet dry

Wear boots if you're boat-fishing. A boat deck can get very slippery and a rogue wave can easily make you lose your balance. Sneakers might be more comfortable – but not when a wave has washed over the side and soaked them. Fishing all day with cold, wet feet will take the fun away.

That sickly feeling

Being seasick is a horrible feeling. If you're one of the lucky ones who don't suffer, be sympathetic to those who do. There are all sorts of claimed remedies, from ginger tablets to staring at the horizon, from having a big breakfast to not having a breakfast. It's worth avoiding alcohol the night before and drinking plenty of water, as well as staying away from the smell of diesel. Avoid enclosed spaces (don't be tempted to go inside a cabin) and you'll find that the centre of the boat is the most stable if the rolling starts getting to you. Stay away from someone who's being sick. It's very infectious. There is only one remedy that works for everyone, and that's not getting on a boat at all.

Watch out for four-legged beach thieves

When beach-fishing at night, always keep containers and your holdall closed. Foxes can be incredibly cheeky and I know several anglers who have lost cod or sole because a fox has sneaked up and snaffled their catch.

Quick tip

TREAT CUTS AT ONCE
If you cut yourself with line, of a fish spikes you, or a knife slips, wash the cut immediately in sea water. Then put a plaster on it and a dab of antiseptic like Bonjela. Don't think: "I'll sort that out when I get home." Always carry a few plasters.

Top 10

extraordinary shark world records

1 101lb hammerhead on 6lb line

2 119lb blue on 2lb line

3 160lb 12oz tiger on 4lb line

4 260lb 5oz thresher on 20lb line

5 342lb mako on 6lb line

6 382lb porbeagle on 16lb line

7 385lb whaler on 16lb line

8 652lb 8oz mako on 12lb line

9 839lb tiger on 16lb line

10 1068lb great white on 20lb line

Beating the crabs

Pestered by crabs? Use flotation beads. These will keep your rig off the bottom and mean that the fish have a chance to get at the bait before crabs have stripped the hook. These beads are also a good idea to use at slack water.

Don't believe the stories that crabs won't eat crab bait. They will. And they will strip a worm-laden hook quickest of all. Tougher baits like squid, mussel, whelks, and razorfish will last longer, and a side cut from a frozen bait also has a better chance of surviving long enough for fish to find it.

Mastering mullet

Mullet are probably the toughest sea fish of all to catch. They are generally easier to catch when you can't see them. You'll find that certain methods work well in certain areas, and transferring these to other areas rarely proves as successful.

You can catch them on all sorts of baits (I've had them on ham fat, chunks of mackerel, sand ragworm, maggots, bread, a baited spoon, and carp pellets) but the big lessons are: use small hooks, fish light line (I've used as light as 1.5 kg/3 lb) and get the bait right. Groundbaiting seems to work well if you're fishing where they stop to feed, like outfalls and around pier structures. Trying to intercept them as they come in with the tide (you will often see mullet in under 30 cm (1 ft) of water) is a waste of time.

If fishing for mullet from a pier, you'll often find that there's a critical depth, often between the level where pouting and smelt will feed, that produces most mullet.

LEARN TO PUMP

Fishing for big-game fish like marlin, tuna, or even skate? Then you need to learn how to pump a fish, using your back muscles rather than your arms. A shorter rod will give you more leverage.

The last few seconds

Ease off the drag when you have a big fish close to the boat. Its last lunges are often the time that you will lose a fish.

Uptiding tips

Uptiding is a brilliant method for catching more fish in water up to 18-21 m (60-70 ft). After that, it loses its effectiveness. The method, popularised by John Rawle and Bob Cox off the port of Bradwell, was designed for fishing the shallow water around this area of the Essex coast. They found that using a grapnel lead and casting uptide and away from the boat intercepted fish that seemed to move away from the anchored boat.

When you use this method, you're looking not for the rod top to pull down, but for 'dropback' bites, where a fish dislodges the lead. The right sort of rod is important here. Too stiff, and it will pull out the weight. Too soft, and the rod bounces around too much. Special uptiding rods are cheap and a good investment. I've used my uptiders in The Gambia and for mahseer in India!

Go light for gar

Garfish will give you great sport as long as you don't fish heavy. A line of 2.5-3.5 kg (6-8 lb) is adequate. You can catch them only a few feet from the surface. A bunch of two or three small ragworm, fished on a short-shank hook about size 6 or 8, can work well, but the best bait is a thin sliver of mackerel. Cut this with a razor blade, and use only the silver part of the fish. Cut off as much of the flesh as you can, leaving only a very fine layer of flesh of less than 1 cm (½ in). Hook this in the very end, so that it moves in the tide like a small fish.

You can use garfish for bait if you can't get mackerel. They make a better strip bait than herring, though not as good as mackerel. Though they've got green bones, they aren't bad to eat, but the trend nowadays is to return all sea fish unless you're going to eat them. For goodness' sake, don't take them home to feed a cat. Our fish are worthy of more than that miserable fate. In particular, return small bass. They are slow-growing, so taking school bass is damaging future sport.

Draw for boat places

Unless you're fishing on a boat with friends, it's much fairer to draw for where you'll fish because, unless you're uptiding, those at the stern of the boat are generally in the most favourable position. I think the idea of changing position halfway through the day, with everyone moving round a few places (depending how many are fishing) is also a fair system.

Dull your leads

We tend to think of sea fish as far less cautious than freshwater ones, but they can still be scared off. A shiny new lead weight will often make them wary. Soak your leads in vinegar before you fish and this will take the shine away.

Quick tip

WD-40 TO CATCH FISH
Nobody seems to know why, but a squirt of WD-40 onto your bait seems to bring more bites!

Circle hooks

The trend in the US and elsewhere is to use circle hooks which are more efficient at hooking fish and keeping them on, but are far less likely to deep-hook fish. Give them a try for ordinary fishing. I've only been using them for a while, but my results seem to be better.

Try the fly

If you're not too concerned with catching the biggest fish in the sea, try fly-fishing for bass, mackerel or pollack. The fight is tremendous on a fly rod, and you can keep fit by just taking a rod and a box of flies. You can have just as much fun with a box of lures and a spinning rod. Again, keep on the move until you find fish.

Alfred Dean holds the record for the heaviest fish ever caught and listed by the International Game Fish Association (IGFA). On April 21, 1959 he caught a 2,664 lb great white shark off the coast of south Australia. Amazingly, he subdued this monster in only 50 minutes on 130 lb line.

Beach safety

When beach-fishing, it's tempting to wear chest waders to gain a few extra yards. Yes, you can achieve more distance, but you need to watch out for undertow. With chest waders, you're far less able to scramble back to the beach, and the temptation is always to try to edge further and further out. Learn to cast better in the first place!

Making bait go further

The quality of dried bait has improved tremendously. Fresh is always best, but a few tubs of dried ragworm or lugworm will store for ages and can give you emergency bait when you're running out. Mix with fresh bait to make the fresh stuff last longer.

To freeze black lug, wrap each worm individually in Clingfilm to get all the air out before freezing. If you put it in newspaper, it will dry out.

Quick tip

TIE UP TRACES THE NIGHT BEFORE
Save yourself a lot of trouble by tying traces before you go fishing. Keep them in a rig wallet. If the trace gets damaged on rocks or by a fish's teeth, you can change it in seconds. Competition fishermen bait up a whole rig so that they can just clip off the one they have just retrieved, put on the new one and cast out straight away. You don't catch fish when the rig is out of the water!

An early peel

Another time-saving ruse is to peel bait like peeler crabs in advance and soak them in a fish attracting juice like herring oil, pilchard oil, or one of the oily attractors beloved by carp anglers. Keep these in a closed bait box and you have several baits ready to hook straight on, rather than wasting time peeling a new crab.

I won the national sea-fishing title by having my mackerel strip pre-cut so that once I had caught a fish, I could put on a new bait straight away, rather than cutting new ones on the spot.

Cheap pirks

Pirks are probably the best way to catch fish over wrecks, or for those big Norwegian cod and pollack. But they are very expensive to buy. Make your own from old car handles (they cost next to nothing from a breakers yard) or a length of chrome pipe filled with lead.

A boat check

If you're fishing from your own boat, make a check-list of things that you need on every trip. This covers things like life-jackets and flares, spare fuel, spare plug, spanner, mobile phone and GPS, to emergency length of rope, milk for a cup of tea, and waterproofs. Run through this list before you take the boat out. Always check the forecast before you take out your own boat. Don't take risks. If the forecast is for severe weather, don't go out at all or stay in close where you're not in danger.

Flapper for conger

A mackerel 'flapper' is one of the best baits for conger. To prepare it, use a sharp filleting knife and cut out the backbone, starting from the tail end. When you reach the head, just turn the fish over and repeat the process. Take off the tail as well, as this can cause problems with tangles when it spins.

Use a split ring

If you're using a zip-lock boom to attach your lead, you'll find that on weights over 450 g (1 lb), the quick-change adaptor can come undone. To solve the problem replace it with an oval split ring. Changing weights will be a bit harder but you won't lose leads.

Quick tip

A LIFESAVER
Give money gladly to the lifeboat service. One day, it might save your life.

Make your own leads

Save yourself a ton of money by buying a lead-moulding kit. Get one that enables you to change the wires to suit the seabed, or even to fish over rougher ground with no wires at all. Using very long wires will enable you to hold bottom in quite fierce tides, and in certain places (Dover's Admiralty Pier is a good example) you can present a bait that would normally be swept into snags or out of the fish-catching zones. You simply use shorter or less stiff wires as the tide eases.

DON'T FORGET YOUR CRIMPS

Crimps are invaluable for so many situations, and they are essential when you are using wire. Always carry a pair of crimping pliers and keep them well oiled. Saltwater is very destructive and there's nothing more useless than a pair of rusty crimping pliers that won't open.

Keep a record book

If you fish the same area regularly, it will pay dividends to keep a record book. Note down the state and height of the tide when you start getting bites, the barometric pressure and the phase of the moon. Sounds daft, but the moon has a significant effect on fishing, especially at night. You will start to notice a pattern, and you can save yourself hours of dead time (and a lot of crab-attacked bait) by fishing only at the hot periods.

Experienced anglers who live close to the sea and know their patch well will often come out to fish for only one or two hours, knowing that they are unlikely to catch at other times. It's also entertaining reading, if you add a little colour about what you caught (or didn't) years later.

Take care of the fish

If you're fishing from a pier don't throw fish back into the sea from a height. Try to slip them back into the water (assuming you're not going to eat them) or use a dropnet to lower them to the water. Today's catch is tomorrow's breeding stock.

Band your baits

Another useful lesson from carp anglers is the use of bait bands. These plastic circles work very well, especially with circle hooks, for fish like flounders and mullet that suck at a bait. It might look slightly odd with the bait not actually on the hook but attached separately, but it's very effective for close-range fishing. It doesn't work so well at long distance, though you can use PVC to attach the hook and protect it from the resistance of distance casting.

Scents make sense

Sea anglers can pick up some valuable tricks from their freshwater counterparts. One is the use of scent trails to attract fish, either by using a lead with a bait cavity or by adding scent to your bait. You'll also find that adding an attractor to baits when you freeze them will improve your catches. I like to add concentrated crab juice to peelers when I freeze them, though I've heard of anglers catching on all sorts of strange additives, including mango and strawberry!

Go small to catch

Always carry some small hooks with you. In flat-calm conditions, these can draw bites when big baits like untouched. The lesson of big baits for big fish is a very good one, but if you want to catch a few fish, scaling down can mean bites. This doesn't just work for fish like sole and garfish, which have small or narrow mouths. When going for garfish, mackerel, scad or shad, I've always had far more success using size 6 or 8 short-shanked hooks, because they have a better chance of penetrating and allow the bait to move around more naturally.

Top 10

British sea records your children could break!

1. Sea stickleback (4dr)
2. Big-scale sand smelt (5dr)
3. Butterfly blenny (1oz 2dr)
4. Butterfish (1oz 2dr)
5. Rock goby (1oz 4dr)
6. Four-bearded rockling (1oz 7dr)
7. Anchovy (1oz 8dr)
8. Black goby (2oz 4dr)
9. Sand smelt (2oz 9dr)
10. Goldsinny wrasse (3oz 4dr)

Groundbait is not just for freshwater

Groundbaiting also works well for several species, especially mullet. But you can also use this technique for mackerel, garfish, wrasse, conger, tope and even bass, and it's the standard method of attracting sharks. When drifting or fishing from an anchored boat, I have found that small pieces of fish and dead or dying sandeels will draw fish out of a reef or into the drift that you're working.

The Channel Islands anglers use a disgusting mix of bread, fish oil and the kitchen sink, but it seems to work. Bran is a great medium to hold scent if you're not fishing a strong tide flow.

Weight that dropnet...

When using a dropnet (an easy thing to make yourself with a bit of netting and the frame of a cycle wheel), you will find that it is easily swept out of position in a strong tide. The weight of the frame isn't enough, so add weight to the bottom of the net.

...but not a lure

Don't be tempted to add weight to your lures when spinning from beach or rocks. You'll find that the lure does not work as naturally and while it may give you extra yards, you'll snag up a lot more. Use a heavier lure! The only time you need extra weight is with sandeel imitations or unweighted shad lures.

Index

INDEX OF LISTS:

'The Greatest Tips in the World' books

Pet Recipe books

The Greatest Feline Feasts in the World by Joe Inglis
ISBN 978-1-905151-50-9

The Greatest Doggie Dinners in the World by Joe Inglis
ISBN 978-1-905151-51-6

'The Greatest in the World' DVDs

The Greatest in the World – Gardening Tips
presented by Steve Brookes

The Greatest in the World – Yoga Tips
presented by David Gellineau and David Robson

The Greatest in the World – Cat & Kitten Tips
presented by Joe Inglis

The Greatest in the World – Dog & Puppy Tips
presented by Joe Inglis

For more information about currently available
and forthcoming book and DVD titles please visit:

www.**thegreatest**inthe**world**.com

or write to:

The Greatest in the World Ltd
PO Box 3182
Stratford-upon-Avon
Warwickshire CV37 7XW
United Kingdom

Tel / Fax: +44(0)1789 299616
Email: info@thegreatestintheworld.com

The author

Keith Elliott has fished for the British press at match fishing and trout-fishing, as well as being a former winner of the national sea-fishing championships. He has fished all over the world, from the Great Barrier Reef to Mongolia, and caught everything from gudgeon to bonefish, from sharks to salmon. He has written several books on fishing, including *How to be the World's Best Fisherman*, the autobiography of four-times world angling champion Bob Nudd, and the fishing book for the Duke of Edinburgh's award scheme.

One of the first National Anglers' Council coaches, Keith has written a weekly fishing column for The Independent newspaper since 1986, and is editor of Classic Angling, a bi-monthly magazine for collectors of antique tackle and those interested in the history of fishing. He is chairman of the Angling Writers' Association, an organisation that he helped to found in 1999.